Greater Essays

Greater Essays

Keith S. Folse
University of Central Florida

Tison Pugh
University of Central Florida

THOMSON
HEINLE

THOMSON

HEINLE

Publisher: Patricia A. Coryell
Editor in Chief: Suzanne Phelps Weir
Sponsoring Editor: Joann Kozyrev
Senior Development Editor: Kathleen Sands Boehmer
Development Editor: Kathleen M. Smith
Editorial Assistant: Evangeline Bermas
Senior Project Editor: Margaret Park Bridges
Associate Manufacturing Buyer: Brian Pieragostini
Executive Marketing Manager: Annamarie Rice
Marketing Associate: Andrew Whitacre

Cover image: © Illustration Works

Excerpts, page 149, from Kenneth Janda, Jeffrey Berry, Jerry Goldman, and Kevin Hula, *The Challenge of Democracy Brief*, 4/e, © 2002. Excerpts, page 9, from James Birk, *Chemistry*, © 1994. Excerpts, page vii, from Virginia Carr, *Collected Stories of Carson McCullers*, © 1987. Excerpts, pages 10–11, 55, from Keith Folse and Marcella Farina, *College Vocabulary 3*, © 2006. Excerpts, pages 33, 63, 77, from Jean-Paul Valette and Rebecca Valette, *Contacts*, 4/e, © 1989. Excerpts, pages 96–97, 283, 296–297, 371, 375, from Scott Ober, *Contemporary Business Communication*, 4/e, © 2001. Excerpts, back cover, from Laura Chesterton, *Effective Business Communication*, © 1992. Excerpts, page 9, from Jack Moeller, Winnifred Adolph, Barbara Mabee, and Helmut Liedloff, *Kaleidoskop*, 5/e, © 1998. Excerpts, page 163, from Virgil Salera, *Multinational Business*, © 1969. Excerpts, page 191, from John Daly and Isa Engleberg, *Presentations in Everyday Life: Strategies for Effective Speaking*, © 2001. Excerpts, pages xv–xvii, from Larry Benson, Ed., *Riverside Chaucer*, © 1987. Excerpts, pages 22, 235–236, from Keith Folse, Elena Vestri Solomon, and Barbara Smith-Palinkas, *Top 20*, © 2004.

Printed in Canada.

Library of Congress Control Number: 2005938339

Student Text
 ISBN 10: 0-618-26046-3
 ISBN 13: 978-0-618-26046-1

Instructor's Examination Copy
 ISBN 10: 0-618-73143-1
 ISBN 13: 978-0-618-73143-5

3456789-WC-10 09 08 07

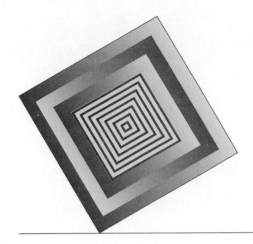

Contents

Unit 2 Process Essays   30

Unit 3 Comparison-Contrast Essays   58

Unit 4 Cause-Effect Essays 92

Unit 5 Persuasive Essays   124

Unit 6   Narrative Essays   157

Appendixes   191

Index   247

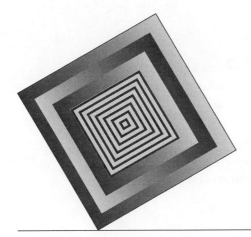

Overview

Greater Essays gives students opportunities to develop their essay writing and language skills. The heart of this book lies in the concept that students will learn to become better writers by learning to become better revisers of their own and of their peers' essays. Professional writers have editors to help them hone their prose. Student writers also need helpful guidance throughout the writing process, from brainstorming and drafting to the final product. To this end, *Greater Essays* models the revision process for students, demonstrating in each chapter an essay's first draft, the draft with teacher's comments, and a final draft that the student has revised in response to the teacher's suggestions. Many writing books address the need for self and peer review, but *Greater Essays* incorporates the revising process into a manageable and effective pedagogical practice.

Because we hope to help students to learn through more engaged revision in *Greater Essays*, we also emphasize the importance of vocabulary for effective essay writing. Quite simply, a high-level vocabulary is essential for effective communication. Numerous studies have documented the decline in vocabulary skills among writing students. *Greater Essays* tackles this incipient problem directly through a series of exercises addressing vocabulary.

In the first unit of *Greater Essays*, we provide a general overview of essays. In the subsequent five units, we discuss in detail five types of essays: process, comparison-contrast, cause-effect, persuasive, and narrative. (These five types may be covered in any order, based on the teacher's preference or students' learning goals.) For each type of essay, we discuss its particular objectives and rhetorical context, as well as providing practice activities in prewriting, revising, organizing, writing effective sentences, and improving grammar skills.

Greater Essays contains a wealth of materials for the classroom, including over 100 activities, six example essays with multiple drafts, and 60 suggestions for additional essay writing assignments.

The three strongest distinguishing features of this book are (1) the multiple drafts of each essay (original student essay, same essay with teacher's comments, the student's revised draft based on the teacher's comments), (2) the connected vocabulary activities, and (3) the five focused grammar points per unit with supporting exercises.

Additionally, we include appendices providing supplementary instruction in such essential areas as sentence types (sentence variety), grammar, and word forms, all of which are challenges to writers at this level.

Excellent writing is a challenge for everyone; even the best of writers will struggle through the process in the never-ending challenge to phrase their thoughts in the most clear and appropriate manner. For students, these challenges can be daunting. *Greater Essays* seeks to alleviate much of the stress of writing through a series of exercises and writing opportunities, but we rely on the teachers in the classrooms to help their students achieve their potential as learners. To that end, *Greater Essays* is a helpful tool, one that we hope you will find useful as you bring forth the best from your students.

Online Study Center

Greater Essays has an Online Study Center website (college.hmco.com/pic/greater-essays1e) for students that provides additional beneficial opportunities for students to learn and practice their new writing skills. Exercises focus on analyzing essay structure, grammar, vocabulary, and writing prompts.

Online Teaching Center

The *Greater Essays* Online Teaching Center (college.hmco.com/pic/greateressays1e) includes a sample syllabus, detailed teaching notes about each chapter, an answer key, and downloadable tests that instructors can administer to students.

ACKNOWLEDGMENTS

We would like to thank our composition colleagues who generously shared their ideas, insights, and feedback on writing, community college and university English course requirements, and textbook design. Because of their input, this book reflects the needs of real teachers in real classrooms.

We offer special thanks to our incredible editors at Houghton Mifflin. Very special kudos go to Susan Maguire, who has been a constant source of guidance and inspiration throughout the work on this book. Susan, your devil's advocate style helped us to reconstruct parts of this text into the work that it has become. We thank you for your fount of ideas and "what if" suggestions, but we are even more thankful for your friendship, your kindness, and your great demeanor. Likewise, we are indebted to Kathy Sands Boehmer, who offered us ideas and feedback and helped us to keep ourselves and this writing project on schedule. In addition, we are indebted to our development editor, Kathleen Smith, whose amazing editing and diligent work have played a major part in this final product.

Thanks are also in order to Jennifer Turner, graduate assistant at the University of Central Florida, for detailed attention and work.

We would also like to thank the following reviewers who offered ideas and suggestions that shaped our revisions: Andrew Barnette, University of Mississippi; Leslie Biaggi, Miami Dade College; Marta Dmytrenko-Ahrabian, Wayne State University; Nicholas Hilmers, DePaul University; Marta Menendez, Miami Dade College; Alan Shute, Bunker Hill Community College; and Wendy Whitacre, University of Arizona.

Finally, many thanks go to our students, who have taught us what composition ought to be. Without them, this work would have no purpose.

Keith S. Folse

Tison Pugh

UNIT

1

An Introduction to Writing Essays

Writing Goal:	To learn about the structure of a five-paragraph essay
Grammar Topic 1.1:	Nouns and Verbs
Grammar Topic 1.2:	Adjectives
Grammar Topic 1.3:	Prepositions
Grammar Topic 1.4:	Confusing words: *a / an*
Grammar Topic 1.5:	Word Parts

WHAT IS AN ESSAY?

ESSAY	a short written composition on one subject that expresses the views of the writer.

What would the world be like if there were no words? Consider how often we think, speak, read, and communicate with words. How would we talk to our family and friends, or how would we fulfill our basic needs for food, shelter, and clothing if we did not have access to language?

We are surrounded every day by the written word, as seen in notes, postcards, letters, instruction manuals, books, e-mail, websites, and newspapers. In this book, we will study how we communicate through essays, which are short written compositions that share our thoughts about a given topic with an audience. Whether that audience is a teacher, fellow students, or the world beyond the classroom, an essay expresses the writer's point of view so that it may be fully understood.

HOW IS AN ESSAY ORGANIZED?

Though essays vary greatly in their subject matter and style of writing, the most common academic essays share a similar structure. They are made up of five paragraphs organized in an **introduction**, a **body**, and a **conclusion**.

INTRODUCTION	Paragraph 1
BODY	Paragraphs 2, 3, 4
CONCLUSION	Paragraph 5

Some common types of academic essays, all of which you will study in this book, include process, comparison-contrast, cause-effect, persuasive, and narrative essays.

WRITER'S NOTE: The Five-Paragraph Essay

When textbooks teach how to write an essay, the most common form that is taught is an essay of five paragraphs. Why is this form emphasized? The five-paragraph essay allows writers great freedom to explain their ideas on a given subject to their readers. At the same time, the traditional assignment in many writing classes is a five-paragraph essay. In addition, if you understand how to write a five-paragraph essay, you can easily expand this structure to include more paragraphs to address increasingly complex and sophisticated ideas.

Activity 1	Reading an Example Essay

Read this five-paragraph essay. Can you identify which paragraphs are the introduction, the body, and the conclusion?

Essay 1

EXAMPLE ESSAY

Against E-Voting

1   Have you ever considered that computers threaten democracy? With computer technology advancing daily, we know that many activities that used to take many long hours can now be <u>accomplished</u> in a few minutes, or even seconds. For the most part, these technological <u>innovations</u> promise to save us time and money and to make our lives easier and more comfortable. Despite the greater efficiency of computers in so many areas, we should not turn over all

EXAMPLE ESSAY

aspects of our lives to computers. In particular, I believe that we should not vote with computers or other electronic media because democracy is too important to <u>cede</u> to the unreliability of cyberspace.

2   In years past, people voted on paper ballots and marked them with ink or some similar means. Voters could see the choices they made. They could look back over their ballot to ensure that they did not make a mistake. Also, if arguments <u>arose</u> over the outcome of an election, paper ballots allowed election officials to count votes by hand. This process may be <u>tedious</u>, but it has the benefit of being <u>verifiable</u>. Several areas of the country still use this system of voting, and it provides a crucial foundation for ensuring fairness.

3   Without this traditional system of voting, however, voters do not really know whether their votes are <u>tallied</u> accurately on e-voting systems. It is quite possible that a computer technician could develop a program so that a person could select one candidate on a computer screen, yet the vote would be counted for another candidate. Although some people might think this scenario sounds <u>paranoid</u>, consider how many stories you hear in the news about <u>breaches</u> in computer security. The simple fact is that <u>hackers</u> can gain access to many computer systems for illegal purposes. By illegally entering into a cyber-<u>polling</u> station, they could easily change the outcome of an election.

4   If voting commissions decide to use these electronic voting machines in their districts, they would be well advised to ensure that all voters receive receipts for their votes that would then be collected for subsequent verification. In this manner, voters could make sure that their receipts stated clearly that they did in fact vote for the candidates they desired. Furthermore, if any candidate suspected that the election was unfair, these receipts could be counted by hand and checked against the results that the computers provided.

5   Computer technologies have improved the qualities of our lives vastly, but these technologies are not a <u>panacea</u> for all of society's troubles. Sometimes a little more human work ensures a better result. Since voting is critically important to the effective and honest working of democracy, we should rely on a much older technology—paper and ink—rather than on computers for all of our elections.

accomplished: completed

innovations: new ideas or systems

cede: yield

arose: came into being, appeared

tedious: tiresome, boring

verifiable: able to be proven true or accurate

tallied: listed or recorded

paranoid: irrationally suspicious

breaches: holes

hackers: people who gain access to computer systems to steal information or money

polling: voting

panacea: a cure for all diseases or problems

How Do You Write an Introduction?

INTRODUCTION	1. gives background information 2. presents the topic—the primary subject of the essay 3. includes a thesis statement—the writer's ideas about or position on the topic

The first paragraph of a five-paragraph essay is the introduction. The introduction has three objectives.

1. It gives background information to connect the reader to the topic.

2. It mentions the topic, which is the subject of the essay.

3. The thesis statement summarizes the main point of the essay and explains the writer's idea or position about the topic. In short, the thesis statement gives the writer's plan for the essay.

What Is the Difference Between the Topic and the Thesis Statement?

The topic is the general subject of the essay, while the thesis statement is a specific sentence that explains the writer's position about the topic.

TOPIC	the subject of the essay
THESIS STATEMENT	the writer's position about the topic

All writers must determine why they are writing; they must know what their main idea is and why it is important to them. This idea is contained in a sentence called the **thesis statement**. The difference between a topic and a thesis statement is illustrated in the following example.

Topic: cell phones in high schools

Thesis statement: Student use of cell phones should be prohibited in high schools.

Note that the topic does not show the writer's idea or position. The writer's opinion is contained in the thesis statement.

Working on Thesis Statements

The most important sentence in an essay is the thesis statement. This statement identifies the writer's main idea and tells what points will be explained or supported.

Many excellent thesis statements include an idea about a topic and a reason to support that idea or position. For example, in "Against E-Voting," pages 2–3, the writer's position is "In particular, I believe that we should not vote with computers or other electronic media." The reason to support this position is "because democracy is too important to cede to cyberspace."

Note: Because is followed by subject + verb; *because of* is followed by a noun. This structure is further explained in Grammar Topic 5.3 on page 145.

| Activity 2 | Thesis Statement Ideas, Positions, and Reasons |

For each topic below, complete the thesis statement with an idea or a position. Then add a controlling idea—a reason for supporting the idea or position.

1.   Topic: Humanities

Thesis statement: My favorite author is _____ because _____.

2.   Topic: Sciences

Thesis statement: I want to study _____ because _____.

3.   Topic: Business

Thesis statement: If I could be the president of any company in the world, it would be

_____ because _____.

4.   Topic: Personal

Thesis statement: My favorite recreational activity is _____ because _____.

What Is in the Body of an Essay?

| BODY | 1. usually consists of three paragraphs
2. explains and supports the thesis statement |

The body of the essay follows the introduction. In the body paragraphs, writers explain and support their ideas or position from the thesis statement. In a good essay, the body paragraphs develop the writer's thesis statement so that the reader fully comprehends the writer's point of view.

Transition Words

One way to make the supporting information in the body paragraphs clear is to use transition words. Transition words help the reader to follow the ideas in the essay. They can be single words such as *but*, *this*, and *although*. Transitions can also be phrases such as *in addition*, *as a result*, and *for these reasons*.

Two words that are especially helpful for connecting ideas in your writing are *this* and *these*. You can mention an idea in one sentence and then refer to it in subsequent sentences using the words *this* or *these*. Using *this* or *these* helps readers to know that you are talking about the same continuing topic.

Two Transition Examples from "Against E-Voting"

1. In paragraph 2, the writer talks about the advantages of traditional voting systems. Paragraph 3 addresses the ways in which e-technologies can be exploited and thus circumvent honest voting practices. It is important to study how the writer moves from paragraph 2 to paragraph 3. The writer does not start talking directly about e-voting fraud in paragraph 3. Instead, the writer says "Without *this* traditional system of voting, however, voters do not really know whether their votes are tallied accurately on e-voting systems." Here the word *this* is used as an adjective before the noun *system*.

2. In paragraphs 2, 3, and 4, the writer explains why computer technologies create some serious problems. At the beginning of paragraph 5, the conclusion, the writer argues that "*these* technologies are not a panacea for all of society's troubles." Instead of repeating all the facts or reasons again, the writer uses the "umbrella" word *technologies* preceded by the adjective *these*.

WRITER'S NOTE: Using *this* and *these* with Noun Synonyms

The purpose of *this*, *that*, *these*, and *those* is to avoid repeating the same noun. Although these four words can function as pronouns or as adjectives, it is preferable to use them as adjectives in academic writing to ensure clarity. Using them as adjectives requires you to use a different noun, a synonym, instead of repeating the same noun. This strategy makes your writing sound more academic.

original noun
↓
Hackers can gain access to many computer systems for illegal purposes.

transition word   synonym
↓   ↙
These criminals could easily change the outcome of an election.

Activity 3	*This* and *These*

Write this *or* these *on the line to show the second reference to a noun. The first one has been done for you.*

1. A huge number of European immigrants entered the country in the late 1800s. Many of ____*these*____ people came from Ireland and Italy.

2. The flag of the United States has stars and stripes on it. _____ symbols represent the states and the original colonies.

3. In our history class today, we read about the Civil War. _____ war lasted from 1861 to 1865 and resulted in the deaths of millions of citizens.

4. The first step in making potato salad is to peel six potatoes. Once _____ step has been completed, you will boil the potatoes for fifteen minutes.

5. According to a report in the newspaper yesterday, the president has suggested that university education should be free for certain students. _____ proposal is extremely popular with the parents of _____ students. However, _____ story did not say how the president intends to pay for _____ plan.

What Does the Conclusion of an Essay Do?

CONCLUSION	1. summarizes the writer's main point 2. usually offers a suggestion, opinion, or prediction

Most good essays end with a conclusion that summarizes the writer's thesis statement. In the conclusion, a writer does not add any new information. The conclusion often ends with a sentence that expresses a suggestion, an opinion, or a prediction. Without a conclusion, essays often seem incomplete and unfinished.

STEPS IN WRITING A FIVE-PARAGRAPH ESSAY

Step 1	CHOOSING A TOPIC
Step 2	BRAINSTORMING
Step 3	OUTLINING
Step 4	WRITING THE FIRST DRAFT
Step 5	PEER EDITING
Step 6	REVISING YOUR DRAFT
Step 7	PROOFING THE FINAL PAPER

Step 1: CHOOSING A TOPIC

Every essay addresses a specific topic, whether it is one that you choose or one that your teacher assigns. After the topic has been selected, your next task will be to develop ideas about that topic. In this explanation of the seven steps in writing an essay, the topic that we will use is "Computers have a negative influence on society."

WRITER'S NOTE: Don't Write—THINK!

Many writers make the mistake of trying to write an essay without thinking. The first part of writing is not writing; it is thinking. If you start writing too soon, your essay will be unorganized and unfocused.

Think about your topic. What do you already know about it? What do your readers know about it? What do you need to find out about this topic? Only after you have completed this thinking are you ready to begin writing.

Step 2: BRAINSTORMING

The next step in writing an essay is to generate ideas about your topic by brainstorming. Study this example of brainstorming about the topic "Computers have a negative influence on society." The student thought about some negative influences to explain in the body paragraphs.

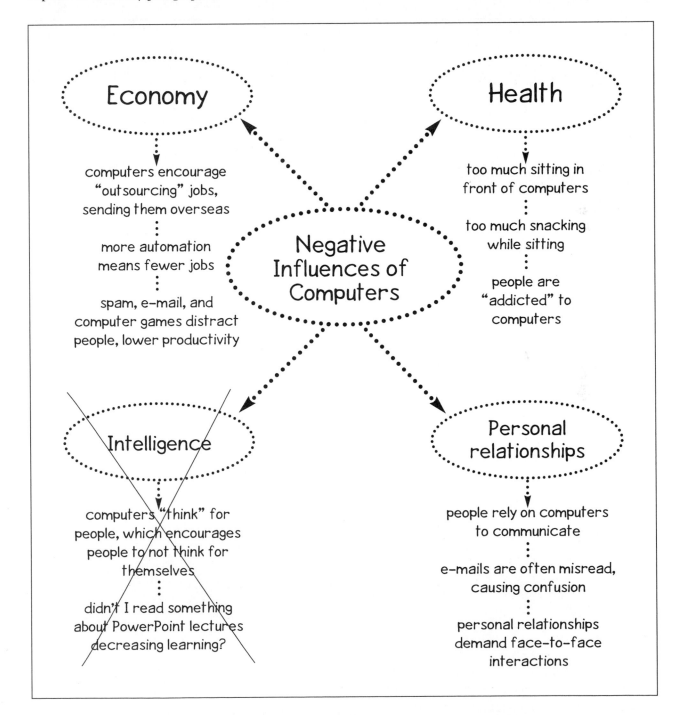

As you can see, the writer came up with four negative influences that computers have. She chose the three that she can present with the best support and crossed out the other.

Activity 4   *Brainstorming a Topic*

Brainstorm in the box below about the following topic: "The government needs to enact, or put into practice, laws to control public use of foul (bad) language." When you are finished, compare your brainstorming with a partner's.

Step 3: OUTLINING

After you brainstorm your ideas, the next step is to make an outline. An outline helps you to organize how you will present your information. It helps you to see which areas of the essay are strong and which are weak.

Formal outlines use Roman numerals, capital letters, and many different levels of information. Some outlines consist of only words or phrases. Others have full sentences. Use the type of outline that will best help you write a great essay.

Here is an example of an outline that uses words, phrases, and sentences.

Topic: Computers have a negative influence on society.

I. Introduction

    A.   Hook (attention-getting sentence; see Writer's Note on page 12)

    B.   Background information

    C.   Thesis statement: *Computers have had a negative impact on society in three significant areas: personal relationships, health, and the economy.*

II. Effects on Personal Relationships

    A.   Topic sentence

    B.   Effect 1

    C.   Effect 2

III. Effects on Health

    A.   Topic sentence

    B.   Effect 1

    C.   Effect 2

IV. Effects on Economy

    A.   Topic sentence

    B.   Effect 1

    C.   Effect 2

V. Conclusion

    A.   Topic sentence

    B.   Brief discussion

    C.   Prediction that with time, these three areas will steadily worsen if the situation continues.

WRITER'S NOTE: Using a Hook to Gain Readers' Attention

Good writers grab their readers' attention with the first sentence of an essay, which is called the hook. A good hook will generate the readers' interest in your essay.

Look at the two versions of a hook below for an essay about a vacation experience. The first hook, which uses the verb *be* (*was*), is simple and boring. The second hook gets readers' attention by providing more details associated with the active verbs *catch*, *lose*, and *get*. Using specific verbs forces the writer to provide interesting details.

Boring hook (be verb):	My worst vacation <u>was</u> in Utah.
Better hook (action verbs):	It might seem unlikely to <u>catch</u> the flu, <u>lose</u> my wallet, and <u>get</u> a speeding ticket in the same week, but these incidents <u>ruined</u> my skiing vacation in Utah.

Activity 5   *Outlining Practice*

Read the outline of "Against E-Voting." Then use the information in the box to complete this outline for the essay.

> - were based on simpler technologies
> - should not be allowed to replace traditional voting technologies
> - some problems but create other problems
> - whether their votes are tallied accurately with electronic voting machines
> - and cons of this compromise position

I. Introduction

     A.   Establish that computers are increasingly common in everyday life.

     B.   Demonstrate that computers solve _____.

     C.   Thesis statement: *We should not vote with computers or other electronic media.*

II. Body Paragraph 1

     A.   Establish that voting practices in the past _____.

     B.   These simpler technologies allow election results to be verified if there is an argument over the results.

III. Body Paragraph 2

    A.   Explain that voters do not really know _____.

    B.   Discuss the threat that hackers pose to supposedly secure computer systems.

IV. Body Paragraph 3

    A.   Address a possible compromise position, in which electronic voting machines provide a "receipt" of a person's vote.

    B.   Discuss briefly the pros _____.

V. Conclusion

    A.   Discuss the ways in which technology cannot solve all human problems.

    B.   Affirm position that electronic voting _____.

WRITER'S NOTE: Peer Editing

A good way to get ideas about improving your writing is to ask a friend or classmate to look at your ideas and your organization, beginning with your outline. If something is not clear to that person, then perhaps you should rework or rewrite that part. Sometimes information is not clear because there is a language problem. Other times, the problem is with unclear ideas or a lack of good supporting ideas. Peer editing is commonly used for rough drafts, but it can also be useful for hooks and outlines and in every step in the writing process.

When you are editing someone else's work, remember to be helpful. If something is not clear, do not write "No." Such a simple remark is not helpful. You should write something like "This sentence is not clear" or "Can you think of three reasons to support this idea?"

The Peer Editing Sheets in Appendix 6 will help you to focus on specific areas to examine in each essay. Here are a few general things that a good peer editor looks at in essays:

- Does every sentence have a subject and a verb and express a complete thought?

- Is there any sentence or section that does not make sense to you?

- Even if you do not agree with the writer's viewpoint, do you understand the writer's line of thinking?

Step 4: WRITING THE FIRST DRAFT

After you have completed your outline and received peer feedback on it, it is time to write the first draft of your essay. Writing an essay is never a linear process. As you write, you will make numerous changes. In fact, you may write the hook or other sentences, rewrite them, and later add additional words until the essay sounds good.

The most important thing in writing a first draft is to write. Too many students spend hours and hours thinking of what they will say. A much better strategy is to get your ideas on the paper and then edit your words to match what you really intend to say.

Step 5: PEER EDITING

Peer editing a draft is a critical step toward the final goal of a polished essay. As the writer of the essay, you will be helped by a fresh perspective because it is difficult for writers to see the weaknesses in their own writing.

Ask a colleague, friend, or classmate to read your essay and to offer suggestions about how to improve it. Some people do not like criticism, but constructive criticism is always helpful for writers. Remember that even professional writers have editors, so do not be embarrassed to ask for help.

Step 6: REVISING YOUR DRAFT

Once you have feedback from a reader, you can use that feedback to improve your essay in the second draft. You have four choices in responding to the feedback:

1. **Do Nothing**

   If you think the writing in your essay is clear enough, then do nothing. However, if one reader had a problem with something in your essay, perhaps other readers will have the same problem.

2. **Add Information**

   If the reader found any unclear language or needed any parts clarified, then you might want to add more information. For example, you might need to add an adjective or identifying information, so instead of writing "the solution is actually quite easy," you could write, "the best solution to this problem that plagues modern society is actually quite easy."

3. **Edit**

   If the reader found any grammatical errors, correct them. Thus, if your draft has several preposition errors, then you should make those corrections. For example, if you wrote, "Computers has had a negative impact on society in three significant area: personal relationships, health, __ the economy," you would edit the sentence in the underlined places to read, "Computers have had a negative impact on society in three significant areas: personal relationships, health, and the economy."

4. Cut Information

If the reader thinks that your writing is wordy or that a certain sentence is not related to the topic, then you should edit out the wordiness or omit the sentence.

Step 7: PROOFING THE FINAL PAPER

Do not forget to proofread! When you proofread, you correct grammar and spelling errors. Careless mistakes make your writing look sloppy and get in the way of clear communication. Even at this late stage, you can add or change words to make your essay sound better. It is essential to proofread your final essay carefully before you turn it in to your teacher.

VOCABULARY FOR BETTER WRITING

Vocabulary is important in any writing. The following activities will help you to improve your knowledge and application of better vocabulary. Activity 6 helps you to build vocabulary word associations. Activity 7 will help you to remember useful combinations of words.

Activity 6   *Improving Your Vocabulary*

Circle the word or phrase to the right that is more closely related to the word on the left. The first one has been done for you.

1. technology	(computers)	briefcase
2. efficiency	quick and fast	fancy and costly
3. media	forms of communication	forms of traveling
4. cyberspace	the World Wide Web	interplanetary exploration
5. ballots	voting	swimming
6. ensure	make certain	make trouble
7. tedious	energetic	time-consuming
8. verifiable	correctable	provable
9. crucial	important	arrogant
10. tallied	characterized	counted
11. scenario	set of circumstances	set of props
12. paranoid	excessively kind	excessively fearful
13. hackers	computer criminals	computer game players
14. receipt	proof of citizenship	proof of a transaction
15. panacea	a cure-all	an essay topic

WRITER'S NOTE: Collocations in Academic Writing

In addition to learning new vocabulary to improve the level of your academic writing, it is important to practice using new vocabulary in examples that sound natural to academic writers. These natural combinations of words are called **collocations**.

Here are two examples of collocations that make the words sound more like advanced or academic writing rather than ordinary conversation:

Example 1: Consider which adjectives can go with the word *imagination* to mean "a very good imagination, the ability to imagine many different things."

"*Even from a very early age, she had a _____ imagination, which certainly led to her later artistic success.*" (Suggested answer: *vivid*. Words such as *big* or *great* are possible, but they sound simplistic and ineffective in academic writing.)

Example 2. Consider which adjectives can go with the word *writer* to mean "producing a lot of works."

"*William S. Porter, better known by his pen name O. Henry, was an extremely _____ writer, publishing over 300 short stories in his lifetime.*" (Suggested answer: *prolific*. Words such as *busy* or *good* are not suitable for academic writing.)

Activity 7   **Using Collocations**

Fill in the blank with the word on the left that most naturally completes the phrase. The first one has been done for you.

1. do / make   _____make_____ a mistake

2. of / by   long hours _____ toil

3. process / part   for the most _____

4. carry / means   with some other such _____

5. from / by   to count votes _____ hand

6. improvement / security   a breach in _____

7. unlikely / quite   it is _____ possible

8. gain / take   _____ access to

9. desire / way   in this _____

10. change / technology   computer _____

11. of / in   all _____ society's troubles

12. about / on   we should rely _____

GRAMMAR FOR BETTER WRITING

This section contains grammar that may be review for you or it may be new. Grammatical errors in essays distract the reader and get in the way of clear communication. Your goal should be to create error-free essays. This section will help you to become a better editor of your own writing. See Appendix 1, pages 192–201, for additional grammar practice.

Grammar Topic 1.1	Nouns and Verbs

The most basic parts of speech are nouns and verbs. A noun names a person, place, feeling, or idea: *doctor, house, sadness, democracy.*

A verb is a word that shows action or state of being: *run, write, think, be, is, does.*

It is often impossible to identify a word as a noun or verb until it is used in a sentence. Consider these examples with *book* and *cook.*

book as a noun:	She purchased a **book** about dinosaurs.
book as a verb:	When did you **book** your flight?
cook as a noun:	He is an excellent **cook**.
cook as a verb:	If you **cook** rice for an hour, it will not taste good.

Certain endings usually indicate whether a word is a noun or a verb. Common noun endings include:

-tion	instruction
-sion	conclusion
-ness	happiness
-ship	friendship
-er	teacher

Common verb endings include:

-ate	donate
-ize	realize
-en	thicken
-ify	clarify
-ed	worked

Grammar Topic 1.1	Nouns and Verbs (continued)

Some endings can be for nouns or verbs. For example, *-s* can indicate a plural noun or a third person singular verb.

verb   *noun*
↓   ↓

He **books flights** for a living.

In addition, *-ing* can end a noun or a verb.

noun   *verb*
↓   ↓

Swimming is her hobby. She is **swimming** in the pool now.

Activity 8 — Working with Nouns and Verbs

Identify each group of words as N *(nouns),* V *(verbs), or* N/V *depending on usage. The first one has been done for you.*

1. __N__ writer, driver, server

2. _____ notify, rectify, beautify

3. _____ redden, widen, sadden

4. _____ conclusion, persuasion, confusion

5. _____ goodness, illness, awareness

6. _____ friendship, championship, scholarship

7. _____ died, cleaned, floated

8. _____ minimize, maximize, summarize

9. _____ dedicate, educate, infiltrate

10. _____ dedicated, educated, infiltrated

11. _____ dedication, education, infiltration

12. _____ dedicating, educating, infiltrating

Grammar Topic 1.2　　　　　　　　　　　　　　　　　**Adjectives**

Adjectives are words that describe nouns or pronouns. Adjectives have many endings, but some common endings are *-y*, *-er* (meaning "more"), *-ed*, and *-ing*.

-y	wind<u>y</u>
-er	cold<u>er</u>
-ed	tir<u>ed</u>
-ing	interest<u>ing</u>

Note: An important point to remember about adjectives is that when they accompany a noun, they occur before the noun.

Incorrect:　The thesaurus offers many synonyms and antonyms **interesting**.

Correct:　The thesaurus offers many **interesting** synonyms and antonyms.

Activity 9　　*Working with Adjective Placement*

Circle the adjectives that modify the underlined nouns. Write C or X to indicate if the word order is Correct or Incorrect.

_____ 1. Because of the confusing <u>address</u>, the package arrived late.

_____ 2. After completing her exam, the <u>student</u> Chinese left the room.

_____ 3. In the last election, the <u>candidate</u> Republican won by a small percentage.

_____ 4. We all agreed that Mark's wedding was a <u>event</u> special.

_____ 5. In Miami, most international <u>flights</u> do not depart early in the morning.

Grammar Topic 1.3   Prepositions

Prepositions are words that show the relationship (often of place or time) between words in a sentence. Prepositions are usually small words, but they are important.

Common prepositions include *at, by, from, in, into, on, for, to, with, after,* and *without.*

A preposition and its noun or pronoun object are referred to as a prepositional phrase: *in May, with my aunt, to Mexico, for five minutes, after the meeting.*

In May, my parents took a trip with my aunt.

Note: to + verb is not a prepositional phrase. It is the infinitive form of a verb: *to go, to swim, to write.*

Activity 10   *Working with Prepositions and Prepositional Phrases*

Underline the prepositions in each sentence and circle the whole prepositional phrase. Hint: The number in parentheses is the number of prepositional phrases in the sentence. The first one has been done for you

1. Everyone agrees that the greater efficiency of computers certainly offers us new possibilities in so many areas of our lives. (3X)

2. Computers are beneficial, but they are tools and we should not turn over all aspects of our lives to computers. (2X)

3. In this particular instance, I believe that we should not vote with computers or other electronic media because democracy is too important to cede to cyberspace. (3X)

4. Without this traditional system of voting, however, voters do not really know whether their votes are tallied accurately on e-voting systems. (3X)

5. The simple fact is that hackers can gain access to many computer systems for illegal purposes. (2X)

6. By illegally entering into a cyber-polling station, they could easily change the outcome of an election. (3X)

Grammar Topic 1.4   **Confusing Words: Articles *a / an***

A and *an* are articles that come before nouns.

    a cat   **an** elephant

Sometimes an adjective comes between *a* or *an* and the noun it modifies.

    a <u>black</u> cat   **an** <u>interesting</u> cat

We use *an* before words that begin with a vowel sound.

    an <u>u</u>mbrella   **an** <u>o</u>pen door   **an** <u>ho</u>nest man

If a word begins with a vowel but not a vowel sound, we do not use *an*. Instead, we use *a*.

    a university   **a** uniform

Activity 11   ***Working with Confusing Words: Articles* a / an**

Fill in the blanks with a *or* an. *The first one has been done for you.*

This paragraph is about Martha Powers. Mrs. Powers is **①** __*an*__ English teacher at Wilson High School. Everyone agrees that she is **②** _____ outstanding teacher. She began her career as **③** _____ teacher at Smith College. After teaching there for five years, she decided to move to **④** _____ high school. She had many reasons for making this decision, but her primary motive was her desire to help young people write better. Mrs. Powers says that this move was **⑤** _____ very difficult decision but that it was **⑥** _____ correct one. During this semester, she is teaching four regular composition courses as well as **⑦** _____ honors composition course. In the future, she may become **⑧** _____ university professor, but for the time being, she is quite happy as **⑨** _____ teacher at Wilson High School. I am certainly happy to be **⑩** _____ student in her course this year.

WRITER'S NOTE: Watch Out for Word Parts!

Word parts include prefixes and suffixes. Prefixes and suffixes change the meaning of the base word. For example, the prefix *un-* changes *happy* to *unhappy*. Suffixes affect the part of speech. For example, *-sion* and *-tion* are usually noun endings (*conclude/conclusion*, *inform/information*), while *-ent* and *-ish* are usually adjective endings (*differ/different*, *style/stylish*).

Mistakes with word parts, especially suffixes, are among the most common writing errors for student writers.

Grammar Topic 1.5	Word Parts

You can increase your vocabulary in two basic ways. One is to learn words that you have never seen before. The second is to learn word parts, which will help you to understand how other words are constructed. Recognizing word parts and using them correctly will increase your vocabulary and thus improve your writing.

Activity 12   *Editing Word Parts*

Read the paragraph. Five of the eight underlined words contain an error with word parts. Correct the error or write C (correct). If you need more information about word parts, review Appendix 3, pages 218–220. The first one has been done for you.

One day, a young boy went to a pizza restaurant to get something to eat. The server said, "May I take your order?" The young boy said, "Yes, ma'am. I would like to order a cheese pizza." The server wrote down this ❶ informing _____information_____, and then she asked what size pizza he ❷ wanted _____. Without ❸ hesitate _____, the young boy replied, "Please bring me a medium pizza." The ❹ serve _____ wrote this down, too, and then walked to the kitchen. A few minutes later, she came back and said, "I just ❺ realized _____ that I forgot to ask you something. The ❻ cooker _____ wants to know if you want your pizza cut into six or eight pieces." The young boy thought about this for a minute and then ❼ answer _____, "Well, I'm not so hungry, so just cut it into six pieces. ❽ Eating _____ eight pieces of pizza would be impossible."

| Activity 13 | *Review of Grammar Topics 1.1–1.5* |

Seven of the ten sentences contain an error involving one of the grammar topics featured in this unit. Write C before the three correct sentences. Write X before the incorrect sentences, circle the error, and write a correction above it.

_____ 1. The manager realized that Kevin had made a honest mistake.

_____ 2. He put the brown socks into the large suitcase.

_____ 3. The first word a sentence in begins with a capital letter.

_____ 4. My son's first pet was a huge cat.

_____ 5. The opposite of happiness is sad.

_____ 6. If you want to rectify this problem, you should call the company at once.

_____ 7. For travel international, it is necessary to have a valid passport.

_____ 8. The next train to Paris departs on six o'clock.

_____ 9. The invention of the telephone was certainly an event important in human history.

_____ 10. Please put the card into the machine for withdraw money.

| **Activity 14** | *Editing a Paragraph: Review of Grammar Topics 1.1–1.5* |

Seven of the ten underlined words or phrases in this paragraph contain an error involving one of the grammar topics featured in this unit. Correct the errors on the lines. If the word or phrase is correct, write C.

One of the most ❶ confuse _____ aspects of the English language is

the use of homophones. What is ❷ an _____ homophone? Why do

homophones cause ❸ confusion? _____ Homophones are ❹ worded

_____ that sound alike but are spelled differently. ❺ In addition with

_____ different spellings, the words usually have different origins.

Examples ❻ inclusion _____ *to/two/too; hour/our; knew/new; so/sew;*

and *road/rode*. To use the correct word ❼ in _____ the correct time, it is

necessary to know the ❽ meaning _____ of each of the homophones. We

can write "I have two books, too" but not "I have too books, two." Likewise, we can write "I

rode on the ❾ bumpy road _____" but not "I road on the bumpy rode."

❿ In conclude _____, although they sound the same, homophones

cannot be used interchangeably.

STUDENT ESSAY WRITING

In this section, you will go through the seven steps in writing a five-paragraph essay. To review the details of each step, see pages 8–15.

Using the seven steps that follow, write a five-paragraph essay. Your teacher may assign a topic, you may think of one yourself, or you may choose from the suggestions in Step 1. You might need to do research.

Step 1: Choosing a Topic

Suggestions:

Humanities:	What are the advantages of being bilingual in today's society?
Sciences:	Which twentieth-century scientific discovery caused the most change to our daily lives? Explain.
Business:	Corporations have collapsed after top executives used dishonest accounting practices. What types of ethical reforms should be put in place to ensure that these practices end?
Personal Narrative:	Describe your first trip to a zoo, theme park, or other tourist attraction.

Think about a topic that interests you. What do you know about it? What do your readers know? What else do you need to know?

1. What topic did you choose? _____

2. Why did you choose this topic? _____

_____

_____

Step 2: Brainstorming

Use this space to jot down as many ideas about the topic as you can.

Brainstorming Box

```




```

Step 3: Outlining

Prepare a simple outline of your essay.

Title: _____

I. Introduction _____

_____

    A.   Background information _____

_____

    B.   Main subject _____

    C.   Thesis statement: _____

_____

II. Body Paragraph 1

     A.   Topic sentence _____

                 _____

     B.   Supporting details _____

                 _____

III. Body Paragraph 2

     A.   Topic sentence _____

                 _____

     B.   Supporting details _____

                 _____

IV. Body Paragraph 3

     A.   Topic sentence _____

                 _____

     B.   Supporting details _____

                 _____

V. Conclusion _____

         _____

Peer Editing of Outlines

Give your outline to a partner. This space is for your partner to write comments about your outline.

1. Are the supporting paragraphs organized in a logical manner? If not, what suggestions do you have?

   _____

   _____

   _____

2. Is there anything in the outline that looks unclear to you? Give details here.

   _____

   _____

   _____

3. Which area of the outline could most benefit from further development? Give at least one specific suggestion.

   _____

   _____

   _____

4. If you have any other ideas or suggestions, write them here.

   _____

   _____

   _____

Step 4: Writing the First Draft

Use the information from Steps 1–3 to write the first draft of your five-paragraph essay.

Step 5: Peer Editing

Exchange essays with someone else. Read that person's essay and offer feedback on Peer Editing Sheet 1, pages 235–236.

Step 6: Revising Your Draft

Read the comments on Peer Editing Sheet 1 about your essay. Then reread your essay. Can you identify places where you plan to revise? List what you are going to do.

1. _____

_____

2. _____

_____

3. _____

_____

Use all the information from the previous activities to write the final version of your paper. Often, writers will need to write a third or even fourth draft to express their ideas as clearly as possible. Write as many drafts as necessary to produce a good essay.

Step 7: Proofing the Final Paper

Be sure to proofread your paper several times before you submit it.

TOPICS FOR WRITING

Here are ten topics for additional writing.

TOPIC 1 ➡ Explain why you would rather live in the city, in the suburbs, or in the country.

TOPIC 2 ➡ If you won $25,000, explain how you would spend it and why.

TOPIC 3 ➡ Who was your favorite elementary school teacher? Why?

TOPIC 4 ➡ If you could attend a major sports championship game, which would you choose to attend and why?

TOPIC 5 ➡ Do you want to have many children? Why or why not?

TOPIC 6 ➡ Describe your best birthday ever. Why was this particular birthday special to you?

TOPIC 7 ➡ Which charity organization would you most like to support? Why?

TOPIC 8 ➡ Reality TV programs are very popular. Why do you think they are so popular?

TOPIC 9 ➡ What was the best gift that you gave or received? What made this gift special?

TOPIC 10 ➡ If you were the mayor of your city, what law would you pass first? Why?

Online Study Center   For additional activities, go to the *Greater Essays* Online Study Center at http://esl.college.hmco.com/pic/greateressays1e

UNIT

2

Process Essays

Writing Goal:	To learn how to write a five-paragraph process essay
Grammar Topic 2.1:	Subject-Verb Agreement
Grammar Topic 2.2:	Apostrophes
Grammar Topic 2.3:	Modals
Grammar Topic 2.4:	Confusing Words: *you're / your*
Grammar Topic 2.5:	Word Parts

WHAT IS A PROCESS ESSAY?

A process essay explains in detail how a certain objective is accomplished. You might think of a process essay as a set of instructions explaining the most effective means to achieve a desired result. The writer believes that the method described is the best way to accomplish the objective.

Although all process essays describe how to accomplish a particular goal, the more interesting essays also include relevant information about the wider context of the process. Why is this process important? How is it useful to the reader who is learning about it? What are the benefits and/or limitations of the process? When you answer such questions as these before you write the essay, your writing will be better tailored to your specific audience.

When you write a process essay, you need to pay special attention to your audience. Are your readers experts in the field? How much information do they need so that they can understand the process? For example, if you write an essay describing DNA splicing, it is quite important to know whether your readers are doctors of biology or high school freshmen.

HOW IS A PROCESS ESSAY ORGANIZED?

The two most common ways of organizing a process essay are **chronologically** and **by priority**.

- In a **chronological process essay**, the writer describes the steps in the order in which they should be performed. This method is helpful for teaching a person a new skill, such as how to tie shoes or how to change the oil in a car.

- In a **priority process essay**, the writer organizes the steps in order of most important to least important. This method is useful for teaching a new concept, such as diplomacy in a foreign country.

TOPICS FOR PROCESS ESSAYS

What is a good topic for a process essay? Process essay topics can range from something as simple as how to boil an egg to something as complex as how to construct a house.

| Activity I | Identifying Topics for Process Essays |

Read these eight topics. Put a check (✓) next to the four that could be good topics for process essays.

_____ 1. the steps in applying for a bank loan to purchase a vehicle

_____ 2. Hawaii versus Florida as a vacation destination

_____ 3. how to get a passport most efficiently

_____ 4. ways to convince citizens to support a candidate

_____ 5. an analysis of driving routes in a certain community

_____ 6. reasons for stopping smoking

_____ 7. an argument against illegal immigration

_____ 8. teaching children to paint

Can you think of two additional topics that would be excellent for a process essay?

9. _____

10. _____

Many of the apparently simple things that we do every day, such as paying bills and cooking meals, involve processes with many steps.

Activity 2   **Brainstorming Steps in a Process**

Choose one task and use the space below to brainstorm the steps necessary to perform it. Then read your steps to a partner to check whether you included them all.

1. directing someone to a building on the other side of campus

2. making your lunch

3. washing your clothes

4. taking care of your pet

STUDYING A SAMPLE PROCESS ESSAY

In this section, you will study three versions of a five-paragraph process essay: a rough draft, the same rough draft with teacher comments, and the revised essay.

Activity 3   *Warming Up to the Topic*

Answer these questions individually. Then discuss them with a partner or in a small group.

1. What is the difference in meaning between *bargain* as a noun and *bargain* as

    a verb? _____

    _____

    _____

    _____

2. Have you ever bargained to buy something? Describe the experience.

    _____

    _____

    _____

3. Write two or three important things that you must do to bargain for the best
    price. What is one thing that you must avoid doing?

    You must: _____

    _____

    _____

    Avoid: _____

    _____

Activity 4   **First Draft of the Essay**

As you read this rough draft, look for areas that need improvement.

Essay 2A   **A Bargain**

As we all know, bargaining is a <u>tough</u> business. The buyer wants to take a product at the lowest possible price. The seller wants to maximize the <u>potential</u> for <u>profit</u>. The desires of the buyer and the seller really oppose each other. It is in the best interest of these people to <u>strategize</u> exactly how they will convince a seller to low his prices. Although prices are <u>inflexible</u>, it never hurts to attempt to bargain with the seller.

Always assume that the price tag represents the starting point of you're negotiations, not the final word on the matter. I am usually very good at bargaining. You might to begin by asking the salesperson whether any sales or discounts will soon be announced. If you do not ask for a special deal, the salesperson probably will not <u>volunteer</u> to give you one. Since salespeople often work on <u>commission</u>, is frequently to their advantage to hide this information from you.

Another thing, you must be prepared to walk away from an item when you are bargaining. Even if you really want it. It's important that you never let sellers to know that you really want their products.

Finally, patience. Looking for bargains take the time and the energy. Sometime you might need to <u>break down</u> and buy a product at a more expensive price simply because you do not have the time necessary for shop any more. Whenever that happens, remember that your time is important, too, and sometimes it is worth spend a little extra money. Especially if you really desire the item.

A best <u>aspect</u> of bargain-hunting is that it is a lot of diversion, and at the same time, it is cheap. Why pay more in something you can buy for less? If you practice your bargaining skills often, you will <u>get better at</u> it and will have more money to bargain with the next time you go shopping.

---

tough: difficult

potential: capacity for growth, development, or coming into existence

profit: money made from a business activity

strategize: make a plan of action

inflexible: rigid, refusing to change

volunteer: give something of one's own free will

commission: money in the form of a fee or a percentage

break down: stop resisting something

aspect: feature

get better at: become good at

Activity 5   **Teacher Comments on First Draft**

Read the teacher comments on the first draft of "A Bargain." Are these the same things that you noticed?

Essay 2B

This title does not express the content of your essay exactly

(A Bargain)

If we all know this, you have no reason to write the essay   As we all know, bargaining is a (tough business) *better: difficult process*   The buyer wants to (take) a   *wrong word choice*

connect

product at the lowest possible price. The seller wants to maximize the

poor word choice

potential for profit. The desires of the buyer and the seller really oppose each

combine   *who?*

other. It is in the best interest of these people to strategize exactly how they

make plural ———→   *word form*   *sometimes*

will convince a seller to (low) his prices. Although prices are inflexible, it

never hurts to attempt to bargain with the seller.

Add Transition?   *confusing words*

Always assume that the price tag represents the starting point of (you're)

Purpose of this sentence? Cut?

negotiations, not the final word on the matter. (I am usually very good at)

(bargaining.) You might (to) begin by asking the salesperson whether any sales or

better word: advertised

discounts will soon be (announced.) If you do not ask for a special deal, the

salesperson probably will not volunteer to give you one. Since salespeople

word missing

often work on commission, is frequently to their advantage to hide this

information from you.

Add transition

Sounds   Another thing, you must be prepared to walk away from an item when

like conversation —→   *fragment*   *no contraction*

you are bargaining. Even if you really want it. (It's) important that you never let

You need more info. here

sellers (to) know that you really want their products.

fragment   *S-V*

Finally, patience. Looking for bargains take the time and the energy.

Sometim(e) you might need to break down and buy a product at a more

expensive price simply because you do not have the time necessary (for) shop any more. Whenever that happens, remember that your time is important, too,

fragment

and sometimes it is worth (spend) a little extra money. Especially if you really

wrong word

(desire) the item.

article error   *hunting for bargains*   *wrong word*

(A) best aspect of (bargain-hunting) is that it is a lot of (diversion,) and at the

?   *prep.*

same time, it is cheap. Why pay more (in) something you can buy for less? If

you practice your bargaining skills often, you will get better at it and ~~will~~

have more money to bargain with the next time you go shopping.

Bargaining does not have a
cost, so it can't be cheap

I enjoyed reading your content. You sound like a tough bargainer!
Good first draft. Your introduction and conclusion are good. Work on the title. Work
on paragraph 3—it needs more development. All body paragraphs should begin with a
transition. You must proofread your paper for fragments! Three fragments in one
essay are too many.

Read the revised version of the essay, now titled "Getting the Best Deal." What has been changed? What still needs improvement?

Essay 2C   **Getting the Best Deal**

Bargaining is a difficult process. The buyer wants to purchase a product at the lowest possible price, but the seller wants to maximize the potential for profit. The desires of the buyer and the seller <u>unequivocally</u> oppose each other, and thus it is in the best interest of buyers to strategize exactly how they will convince sellers to lower their prices. Although prices are sometimes inflexible, it never hurts to attempt to bargain with the seller.

<u>First</u>, always assume that the price tag represents the starting point of your negotiations, not the final word on the matter. Assuming that the price tag is the final price of an item is the single worst mistake that a shopper can make in the bargaining process. You might begin by asking the salesperson whether any sales or discounts will soon be advertised. If you do not ask for a special deal, the salesperson probably will not volunteer to give you one. Since salespeople often work on commission, it is frequently to their advantage to hide this information from you.

<u>Second</u>, you must be prepared to walk away from an item when you are bargaining, even if you really want it. This step in the bargaining process requires determination and good acting skills, but it can pay off financially. It is important that you never let sellers know that you really want their products. At street markets and festivals, <u>scout out</u> the booths first to see

whether anything interests you. If you go back to buy at the end of the day, the sellers will often give you discounts so that they will have fewer products to pack up.

Finally, be patient. Looking for bargains takes time and energy. Sometimes you might need to break down and buy a product at a more expensive price simply because you do not have the time necessary to shop any more. Whenever that happens, remember that your time is important, too, and sometimes it is worth spending a little extra money if you really want the item. However, if waiting two weeks or even two months saves you a considerable amount of money, then it is worthwhile to wait.

Hunting for bargains is a lot of fun, and at the same time, it can save you a great deal of money. Once you start bargaining, you may find that it becomes an addictive game in which you are competing with the salesperson for your money. If you practice your bargaining skills often, you will get better at it and have more money to bargain with the next time you go shopping.

unequivocally: without a doubt, clearly
scout out: investigate
considerable: large, great
worthwhile: valuable, sensible

Analyzing Content and Organization

Activity 7

Analyzing the Content

Answer these questions about the revised version (2C) of "Getting the Best Deal."

1. Is this a chronological or a priority process essay? _____

2. Why does the writer want to give advice about saving money?

   _____

   _____

3. Write the thesis statement here.

   _____

   _____

4. What specific suggestions does the writer offer about bargain hunting?

   _____

   _____

Activity 8

Analyzing the Organization

Read the outline of "Getting the Best Deal." Then use the information in the box to complete the outline for the essay.

- the end of the day
- patience
- successful bargaining
- effective bargaining skills
- the salesperson's interests

I. Introduction

  A. Economics of shopping: both buyer and seller want to maximize profit

  B. Thesis idea: _____ will help the reader to shop more effectively

II. Body Paragraph 1

  A. Use the price tag as the starting point for negotiations, not as the final word on the price

  B. _____ often are not the same as the buyer's

III. Body Paragraph 2

  A. You should walk away from an item

  B. Best to shop at _____

    1. Salespeople are tired

    2. Salespeople want to make a final sale for the day

IV. Body Paragraph 3

  A. Suggest that _____ is key to bargaining

  B. Sometimes you need to stop bargaining and to buy an item in order to save time

V. Conclusion

  A. Indicate that _____ can be fun

  B. Practice at bargaining helps you to get better and have more money for future bargaining

WRITER'S NOTE: Outlines

The purpose of an outline is to help you, the writer, organize your ideas and include sufficient and logical details that support your ideas. Formal outlines should contain only nouns or only full sentences. Some writers prefer to include nouns, phrases, sentences, or a mixture of these. (Note that the outline for "Getting the Best Deal" includes a mixture. If your instructor has not given you instructions for your outline, choose the system that is most comfortable to you.)

TRANSITIONS AND CONNECTORS IN PROCESS ESSAYS

The most commonly used transitions and connectors in process essays are time words and phrases. A process essay outlines the steps in achieving a goal, so the transitions that are needed are typically words and phrases that indicate sequence.

after	finally	second
after that	first	soon
at first	following from … to …	then
at the same time	immediately following	third
before	last	until
during	later	when
eventually	meanwhile	while

Activity 9   *Using Transitions and Connectors*

Reread the revised version (2C) of "Getting the Best Deal" on pages 38-39. Find and list three transitions or connectors and write the paragraph number after each.

1. _____ ( )

2. _____ ( )

3. _____ ( )

VOCABULARY FOR BETTER WRITING

Vocabulary is important in writing. The following activities will help you to improve your knowledge and application of better vocabulary.

Activity 10   *Improving Your Vocabulary*

Circle the word or phrase to the right that is most closely related to the word on the left. The first one has been done for you.

1. bargaining	(buying)	producing
2. maximize	make bigger	make more difficult
3. potential	possibility	practicality
4. desires	wishes	fears
5. unequivocally	completely	almost
6. strategize	plan	capitulate
7. convince	lose	persuade
8. inflexible	soft	firm
9. attempt	formulate	try
10. negotiations	discussions	commands
11. discounts	lower prices	higher prices
12. volunteer	offer	decline
13. commission	a payment	a bribe
14. festivals	celebrations	sufferings
15. scout	smell	hunt
16. stalls	booths	mistakes
17. products	merchandise	leftovers
18. expensive	cheap	costly

44 Unit 2—Process Essays

Activity 11 — Using Collocations

Fill in the blank with the word on the left that most naturally completes the phrase. The first one has been done for you.

1. at / in   purchase a product _____at_____ the lowest price possible

2. about / for   potential _____ profit

3. another / other oppose each _____

4. of / with   in the best interest _____ buyers

5. around / with   to bargain _____

6. of / after   the starting point _____ your negotitions

7. on / under   final word _____ the matter

8. whether / that   ask the salesperson _____

9. for / over   if you do not ask _____ a special deal

10. in / on   work _____ commission

11. around / from   hide this information _____ you

12. away / to   walk _____ from

13. out / forth   scout _____

14. of / in   at the end _____ the day

15. for / in   looking _____ bargains

16. at / in   _____ a more expensive price

17. at / on   _____ the same time

18. of / on   a lot _____ money

GRAMMAR FOR BETTER WRITING

This section contains grammar that might be review for you or it might be new. Grammatical errors in essays distract the reader and get in the way of clear communication. Your goal should be to create error-free essays. This section will help you to become a better editor of your own writing. See Appendix 1, pages 192–201, for additional grammar practice.

Grammar Topic 2.1	Subject-Verb Agreement

In any sentence, the subject and verb must agree in number. This means that a singular verb must be used with a singular subject and a plural verb must be used with a plural subject.

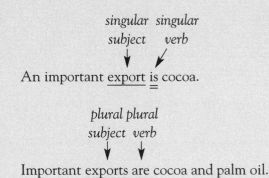

singular singular
subject   verb

An important <u>export</u> <u>is</u> cocoa.

plural plural
subject verb

Important <u>exports</u> <u>are</u> cocoa and palm oil.

Words that come between the subject and the verb can sometimes cause writers to choose the wrong number for the verb. Remember that the object of a preposition is never the subject of a sentence.

singular subject   *objects of preposition*   *plural verb*

Incorrect: The main <u>export</u> of **Honduras, Guatemala, and Colombia** <u>are</u> coffee.

singular subject   *singular verb*

Correct: The main <u>export</u> of **Honduras, Guatemala, and Colombia** <u>is</u> coffee.

| **Activity 12** | *Working with Subject-Verb Agreement* |

Write the correct form of the verb in parentheses.

1. (react)   After horrendous events, people often _____ quite

    differently.

2. (type)   The secretary for our two departments _____ over

    75 words per minute.

3. (export)   Most of the countries in OPEC _____ millions of

    dollars worth of petroleum each day.

4. (reveal)   Surprisingly, our company has found that a survey covering more than one

    hundred colleges often _____ as much information as

    a survey of five key colleges in the central part of the state.

5. (live)   The characters in O. Henry's *The Gift of the Magi* _____

    very simple lives.

| **Grammar Topic 2.2** | **Apostrophes** |

The apostrophe has two main uses in English.

1. The apostrophe shows possession: *Susan's, today's*

2. The apostrophe is used in contractions in place of a letter or letters that have been omitted: *can't (cannot), shouldn't (should not)*

Contractions are not common in academic writing. While it is acceptable to write *I'm* or *don't* in informal writing such as e-mails and postcards, it is less acceptable in formal essays. One place where you might see contractions in essays, however, is in narrative writing.

An extremely common error occurs when apostrophes are used to make plural forms. This is never correct.

Incorrect: For some writers, **apostrophe's** are difficult to understand.

Correct: For some writers, **apostrophes** are difficult to understand.

WRITER'S NOTE: Contractions

Contractions are not used in formal academic writing. Jokes are usually told in informal spoken language—the kind spoken between friends—so a printed joke can have contractions to simulate spoken language.

Activity 13   *Working with Apostrophes*

Read this joke. Add apostrophes where necessary. Be prepared to explain your choices.

An antique collector with lots of money was walking in the downtown area of a city one day.

He saw a small, skinny cat on the sidewalk. The cat was drinking some milk from a small dish.

The antique collector looked again at the dish. What the antique collector saw shocked him.

The cats small dish was extremely old, and the antique dealer knew at once that it was very

valuable. He was so interested in what he had just seen that he immediately walked into the

store to talk to the owner about buying the valuable antique dish. The man did not want the

owner to suspect that the dish was so valuable, so he offered the owner some money for the cat.

He said that he would pay $10 for the cat. The owners answer shocked the man. "No," the

owner said, "I couldnt ever sell this cat." The man was getting

desperate, so he offered the owner a crisp fifty-dollar bill from

his wallet. At this point, the owner could no longer refuse

what the man was offering. Then the man quickly added,

"You know . . . how about including the dish, too? That cat

is probably used to eating from that dish." The owner replied,

"No, sir, Im sorry. You may be right about the cat and the

dish, but that dish is not for sale. "Why not?" asked the man.

The owner answered, "Well, Ill tell you why its not for sale.

You see thats my lucky dish. So far this week, Ive sold fifteen

skinny cats!"

Grammar Topic 2.3   **Modals**

Modals are words used with verbs to express ability, possibility, or obligation. Common modals include *can, could, may, might, must, should, will,* and *would.* Modals also include phrases such as *ought to* and *had better.*

modal
↓
I **should** take that writing class again.

The verb after a modal is always in the base, or simple, form with no inflected ending (*-ing, -ed, -en, -s*). In addition, do not put the word *to* between the modal and the verb.

Incorrect: The solution **might** *lies* in obtaining better raw materials.

Incorrect: The solution **might** *to lie* in obtaining better raw materials.

Correct: The solution **might** *lie* in obtaining better raw materials.

Activity 14   **Working with Modals**

Circle the six modals in this passage. Find the two errors and correct them.

The task of learning and remembering new vocabulary words can be daunting. However, one technique that works for many students is the "key-word method." In this technique, learners must first to select a word in their native language that looks or sounds like the target English word. Then they should form a mental association or picture between the English word and the native-language word. For example, an English speaker learning the Malay word for door, *pintu*, might associating this target word with the English words *pin* and *into*. The learner would then visualize someone putting a "pin into a door" to open it. This could help the learner to remember *pintu* for door. Research on second-language learning shows that this technique consistently results in a very high level of learning.

Grammar Topic 2.4   **Confusing Words: *you're / your***

The words *you're* and *your* sound alike, but they are used very differently. Do not confuse them in your writing.

> *you're* = *you are*: **You're** planning to return these books to the library today.

> *your* = possessive adjective: Can you describe **your** new car to us?

Activity 15   ***Working with Confusing Words: you're/your***

Fill in the blanks with you're *or* your.

You know this situation well. **1** _____ in **2** _____ writing class. **3** _____

teacher gives you **4** _____ assignment. **5** _____ to write an essay describing a

process. Perhaps **6** _____ not quite sure what you will use for your topic. What are

7 _____ options? The topic of any process essay must be one that entails steps.

8 _____ essay should explain these steps. If **9** _____ successful at this, certainly

10 _____ process essay will be a good one.

Grammar Topic 2.5   Word Parts

You can increase your vocabulary in two basic ways. One is to learn words that you have never seen before. The second is to learn word parts, which will help you to understand how other words are constructed. Recognizing word parts and using them correctly will increase your vocabulary and thus improve your writing.

Activity 16   *Editing Word Parts*

Read the paragraph. Five of the eight underlined words contain an error with word parts. Correct the error or write C (correct). If you need more information about word parts, review Appendix 3, pages 218–220. The first one has been done for you.

From the energy ❶ expended _____ C _____ by a hurricane or an earthquake

to the energy ❷ requirement _____ to make an automobile run, energy

affects our lives in ways that are impossible to ignore. Often, when we talk about ❸ energies

_____, we are referring to the energy that people have channeled to provide

heat, light, and ❹ powerful _____ for homes and industries. As the

sources we have ❺ relied _____ on for this energy are depleted or are

found to pose ❻ threatens _____ to our environment, efforts to develop

❼ practical _____ new sources are becoming ❽ intensification

_____.

Activity 17   *Review of Grammar Topics 2.1–2.5*

Seven of the ten sentences contain an error involving one of the grammar topics featured in this unit. Write C before the three correct sentences. Write X before the incorrect sentences, circle the error, and write a correction above it.

_____ 1. If you buy that sweater, your not going to be happy with it.

_____ 2. I don't know where Sammys' coat is; you should ask him.

_____ 3. Pamela thought that the move to Miami would be a wonderful change of

pace, and she was certainly right.

_____ 4. He should does everything in his power to help out his friend.

_____ 5. Pandas eats a diet of bamboo shoots and leaves.

_____ 6. The politicians should all get behind this issue because they know that it

will likely help them get reelected.

_____ 7. It is time for you to face the truth about you're responsibilities.

_____ 8. You're not going to heal if you keep taking the bandage off.

_____ 9. They might to want to help us with our problem, since we might be able

to help them with theirs.

_____ 10. Sitcoms was once very popular on television, but crime dramas are now

the most popular shows.

| **Activity 18** | *Editing a Paragraph: Review of Grammar Topics 2.1–2.5* |

Seven of the ten underlined words in this paragraph contain an error involving one of the grammar topics featured in this unit. Correct the errors on the lines provided. If the word or phrase is correct, write C.

Listening is the communication skill that we use the most. White-collar **❶** <u>workers'</u>

_____ typically devote at least 40% of their workday to listening.

Yet immediately after hearing a ten-minute oral presentation, the average person

❷ <u>retain</u> _____ only 50% of the information. Forty-eight hours later, only

25% of what was heard can be recalled. Thus, listening is probably the least developed of

the four verbal communication skills (writing, reading, speaking, and listening). The good

news **❸** <u>are</u> _____ that you **❹** <u>can improve</u> _____

❺ <u>your</u> _____ listening skills. Tests at the University of Minnesota

❻ <u>shows</u> _____ that **❼** <u>individual's</u> _____ who

receive training in listening improve their listening skills by 25% to 42%. To learn to listen

more effectively, whether **❽** <u>your</u> _____ involved in a one-on-one

dialogue or **❾** <u>are</u> _____ part of a mass audience, give the speaker your

undivided attention, stay open-minded, avoid interrupting, and **❿** <u>involvement</u>

_____ yourself in the communication.

STUDENT ESSAY WRITING

In this section, you will go through the seven steps in writing a five-paragraph essay.
To review the details of each step, see Unit 1, pages 8–15.

Activity 19   *Original Process Essay*

*Using the seven steps that follow, write a five-paragraph process essay. Your teacher may assign
a topic, you may think of one yourself, or you may choose from the suggestions in Step 1. You
might need to do research.*

Step 1: Choosing a Topic

Choose a process that you can explain because you know the steps well.

Suggestions:

Humanities:	Write a process essay in which you describe how to write a poem, research a subject in the library, or teach an academic lesson to a group of high school students.
Sciences:	Scientists often write process papers describing how they achieved a particular set of results from an experiment. Write a process essay describing an experiment so that someone could duplicate your results.
Business:	Managers often codify business practices so that standard procedures will be followed across the company. Write a process essay describing the necessary procedure for a key function of a business in which you have been involved, such as advertising, marketing, or selling a product.
Personal Narrative:	Think of your favorite hobby. How would you explain it to a friend who is interested in learning about it? Write a process essay in which you describe the rudimentary skills necessary for your favorite hobby.

1. What topic did you choose? _____

2. Why did you choose this topic? _____

   _____

   _____

Step 2: Brainstorming

Use this space to jot down as many ideas about the topic as you can.

Brainstorming Box

Step 3: Outlining

Prepare a simple outline of your essay.

Title: _____

I. Introduction _____

_____

    A.   Background information _____

_____

    B.   Main subject _____

    C.   Thesis statement: _____

_____

II. Body Paragraph 1

    A.   Topic sentence _____

            _____

    B.   Supporting details _____

            _____

III. Body Paragraph 2

    A.   Topic sentence _____

            _____

    B.   Supporting details _____

            _____

IV. Body Paragraph 3

    A.   Topic sentence _____

            _____

    B.   Supporting details _____

            _____

V. Conclusion _____

_____

Peer Editing of Outlines

Give your outline to a partner. This space is for your partner to write comments about your outline.

1. Is there anything in the outline that looks unclear to you?

_____

_____

_____

2. Can you think of an area in the outline that needs more development? Do you have any specific suggestions?

_____

_____

_____

3. If you have any other ideas or suggestions, write them here.

_____

_____

_____

Step 4: Writing the First Draft

Use the information from Steps 1–3 to write the first draft of your five-paragraph process essay.

Step 5: Peer Editing

Exchange essays with someone else. Read that person's essay and offer feedback on Peer Editing Sheet 2, pages 237–238.

Step 6: Revising Your Draft

Read the comments on Peer Editing Sheet 2 about your essay. Then reread your essay. Can you identify places where you plan to revise? List what you are going to do.

1. _____

_____

2. _____

_____

3. _____

_____

Use all the information from the previous activities to write the final version of your paper. Writers will often need to write a third or even a fourth draft to express their ideas clearly. Write as many drafts as necessary to produce a good essay.

Step 7: Proofing the Final Paper

Be sure to proofread your paper several times before you submit it.

WRITER'S NOTE: Tip for Better Proofreading

One suggestion for better proofreading is to read your essay aloud. Reading aloud forces you to read more slowly, so there is a better chance that you will hear your errors. You will be surprised at how many errors you can find by following this simple advice.

TOPICS FOR WRITING

Here are ten topics for additional process essay writing.

TOPIC 1 ➟ Explain how to study a new language

TOPIC 2 ➟ Explain the process of finding volunteer work.

TOPIC 3 ➟ What are the steps in becoming accustomed to a new job?

TOPIC 4 ➟ Explain how to settle a dispute between two friends.

TOPIC 5 ➟ Explain how to plan for a vacation.

TOPIC 6 ➟ Explain how to find free time for yourself during a busy day.

TOPIC 7 ➟ Describe how to monitor the performance of employees.

TOPIC 8 ➟ Explain the steps to follow to invest in the stock market.

TOPIC 9 ➟ Explain the steps in learning a new hobby.

TOPIC 10 ➟ Describe how to apply for a job.

Online Study Center   For additional activities, go to the *Greater Essays* Online Study Center at http://esl.college.hmco.com/pic/greateressays1e

Comparison-Contrast Essays

Writing Goal:	To learn how to write a comparison-contrast essay
Grammar Topic 3.1:	Comparative Forms *(-er, more / less; as . . . as, the same . . . as)*
Grammar Topic 3.2:	Parallel Comparison
Grammar Topic 3.3:	Non-Count Nouns
Grammar Topic 3.4:	Confusing Words: *than / then*
Grammar Topic 3.5:	Word Parts Practice

WHAT IS A COMPARISON-CONTRAST ESSAY?

A comparison-contrast essay analyzes how two related subjects are similar and different. For example, you might select the Civil War Generals Grant and Lee or a car versus a bicycle for urban transportation. Sometimes the writer includes an opinion about the merits of the subjects being compared.

The subjects that you compare should have some characteristics in common. Have you ever heard the phrase "You should not compare apples to oranges"? This expression suggests that it is best to compare and contrast similar objects. For example, you could write a comparison-contrast essay about the differences between the President and a movie star. However, unless the movie star is running for President (or unless the President is auditioning for a movie), what is the purpose of the comparison? On the other hand, a comparison-contrast essay that addresses which of two candidates running for President a voter should support or which of two actors should be cast in a certain role would have a much more unified focus and a stronger thesis because there is a reason to compare and contrast the two.

Some comparison-contrast essays suggest that one subject is better than the other. Such an essay should still have a thesis. As you will see, the sample essay in this unit models this style in which the writer does not argue that cats are better than dogs. Instead, the writer offers a thesis about the value of comparing and contrasting the two animals.

A comparison-contrast essay can do one of three things.

- It can say that the two subjects are more different than similar.

- It can say that the two subjects are more similar than different.

- It can show how the two subjects share both similarities and differences.

In other words, your essay may focus on comparing, on contrasting, or on both.

HOW IS A COMPARISON-CONTRAST ESSAY ORGANIZED?

There are two basic ways to organize a comparison-contrast essay: **block method** and **point-by-point method**. Both have an introduction and a conclusion, but the body paragraphs are organized differently.

The Block Method

In the block method, you present information about one subject first and then present information about the other subject. The number of paragraphs that you use for each subject separately should be the same. The block method looks like this:

INTRODUCTION	Paragraph 1	• Hook • Background information • Thesis statement
BODY	Paragraph 2	Subject A • Point 1 • Point 2 • Point 3
	Paragraph 3	Subject B • Point 1 • Point 2 • Point 3
	Paragraph 4	Compare or contrast A and B side by side
CONCLUSION	Paragraph 5	Conclusion (Restate the thesis sentence.)

The Point-by-Point Method

In the point-by-point method, one point for comparison is the topic for each body paragraph. The writer discusses both subjects in relation to that one point. The point-by-point method looks like this:

INTRODUCTION	Paragraph 1	• Hook • Background information • Thesis statement
BODY	Paragraph 2	Point 1 • Subject A • Subject B
	Paragraph 3	Point 2 • Subject A • Subject B
	Paragraph 4	Point 3 • Subject A • Subject B
CONCLUSION	Paragraph 5	Conclusion (Restate the thesis sentence.)

TOPICS FOR COMPARISON-CONTRAST ESSAYS

What is a good topic for a comparison-contrast essay? Obviously, it should be two subjects that are related in some way. You must have a logical reason for making the comparison or contrast. What features do the subjects have in common? What features do they not share? Can you develop a thesis by comparing and contrasting their traits?

Here are some general topics that lend themselves well to a comparison-contrast essay:

- your siblings
- your favorite singers
- your favorite TV shows
- courses of study at two different colleges
- two authors who write on a similar topic
- vegetarian and nonvegetarian diets
- two local newspapers
- political parties
- your favorite vacation spots
- two ways of thinking about a topic

Activity 1	Identifying Topics for Comparison-Contrast Essays

Read these eight topics. Put a check (✓) next to the four that could be good topics for comparison-contrast essays.

_____ 1. the steps in applying for a bank loan to purchase a vehicle

_____ 2. Hawaii versus Florida as a vacation destination

_____ 3. buying an SUV or a car

_____ 4. life with or without a baby

_____ 5. an analysis of voting trends in the United States

_____ 6. career choice of teacher or lawyer

_____ 7. fun activities during a snowstorm

_____ 8. the migratory routes of penguins

Can you think of two additional topics that would be excellent for a comparison-contrast essay?

9. _____

10. _____

Topic Details

After you have selected a topic and the two subjects, your job is to identify the similarities and differences between the two subjects. This process will also help you to identify supporting details for your essay.

Activity 2   **Brainstorming Topic Details**

Think about two people, places, or things that could be compared and contrasted. Fill in the general topic, the two items, and lists of their similarities and differences. When you have finished, discuss your ideas with a partner. Then do the same for another pair of items. One example has been provided.

General Topic	1	2	Similarities	Differences
1. my parents	my mom	my dad	1. age 2. food likes/dislikes 3. attitude toward saving money	1. hobbies 2. attention to detail 3. showing affection 4. superstitious
2.				
3.				

STUDYING A SAMPLE COMPARISON-CONTRAST ESSAY

In this section, you will study three versions of a five-paragraph comparison-contrast essay: a rough draft, the same rough draft with teacher comments, and the revised essay.

Activity 3	*Warming Up to the Topic*

Answer these questions individually. Then discuss them with a partner or in a small group.

1. What is a stereotype? _____

   _____

2. Choose a general noun (e.g., *professions*). Then think of categories within that general noun (e.g., *librarians, police, lawyers*) and come up with three stereotypes about the category words (e.g., most *librarians* are serious people).

   General noun: _____

Category	**Stereotype**
a. _____	a. _____
_____	_____
b. _____	b. _____
_____	_____
c. _____	c. _____
_____	_____

3. Do you have a pet or know someone who has a pet? What kind of animal is it?

   How would you describe the pet's character and personality? _____

   _____

   _____

   _____

   _____

4. The two most popular types of pets are cats and dogs. What are the stereotypes

of a cat? _____

_____

What are the stereotypes of a dog? _____

_____

5. On the basis of your experience, do you think these stereotypes are accurate?

Why or why not? _____

_____

_____

_____

_____

_____

_____

_____

_____

_____

_____

_____

_____

_____

6. What are four reasons why people want pets?

_____

_____

_____

_____

_____

_____

_____

_____

Activity 4   **First Draft of the Essay**

As you read this rough draft, look for areas that need improvement.

Essay 3A   **The Truth About the Cats and the Dogs**

I used to think that the dogs were better then the cats as pets. As I was grow up, my family had a lot of the dogs—many kinds—but we never had cats because my father is allergic to it. I always assumed that when I grew up, I would to have a dog as a pet. My life as a pet owner changed one night when the tiny kitten <u>showed up</u> at my door. He was cold, wet, and hungry, and I was afraid him would die on my doorstep if I did not help him. I never saw myself as a cat owner, but now that I am one, I realize that most of the <u>stereotypes</u> about the cats and the dogs are lies.

The cats are suppose to be not good as well as not nice. My cat, however, are very friendly and even a little messy. He always want my attention, which can be annoying at times. I thought that a cat would sleep all day, but my cat is much more energetic then I expected. If he does not go outside to make <u>frolic</u> in the backyard, he starts to behave a bit <u>neurotically</u>.

The people also say that the dogs are more friendlier than the cats, but I remember a couple of the dogs of my family that were not friendly at all. Our Chihuahua was named "Wagster," and he did not like anyone. Every time someone rang our doorbell, he would to bark greatly to scare the visitor away. Once he even bit a little at my grandmother! She never thought that the dogs were friendly after that experience.

My friend Aimee had a cat that was so <u>aloof</u> and distant that I never saw it when I came to visit. When I <u>dropped by</u> her house, the cat always hid itself under a bed.

My friend Jasper has a dog that is almost very friendly. It licks and licks and licks until I wish it were not quite so friendly. Jasper does not live in my hometown now, and he probably does not have any pets now.

How did this stereotypes about the cats and the dogs develop? As with most <u>prejudices</u>, they reflect more about the peoples who express them than about what is true. Both the cats and the dogs make good pets, and they are bad. It all depends on the individual animal.

showed up: appeared, often unexpectedly

stereotypes: conventional or oversimplified ideas or images of something

frolic: play, as a young child or young animal

neurotically: in an unreasonable way

aloof: distant, reserved, or indifferent in manner

drop by: visit, usually unexpectedly or informally

prejudices: unfair judgments or opinions formed before one knows the facts

Activity 5   **Teacher Comments on First Draft**

*Read the teacher comments on the first draft of "The Truth About the Cats and the Dogs."
Are these the same things that you noticed?*

*Don't use THE unless specific—You have many errors like this. I didn't
mark them all.
Edit carefully!*

Essay 3B   **The Truth About the Cats and the Dogs**

I used to think that ~~the~~ dogs were better (then) the cats as pets. As I was

*List examples—
reader* grow up, my family had a lot of ~~the~~ dogs—<u>many kinds</u>—but we never had
needs details

cats because my father is allergic to (it). I always assumed that when I grew up,

I would (to) have a dog as a pet. My life as a pet owner changed one night when

(the) tiny kitten showed up at my door. He was cold, wet, and hungry, and I

was afraid (him) would die on my doorstep if I did not help him. I never saw

myself as a cat owner, but now that I am one, I realize that most of the
too strong—better word: untrue   *Use your dictionary - these are
beginning level adjectives.*
stereotypes about ~~the~~ cats and ~~the~~ dogs are (lies).
Push yourself!
The cats are suppose(e) to be (not good as well as not nice). My cat, however,
S-V
(are) very friendly and even a little messy. He always wan(t) my attention, which
Details: give an example or two of the times
can be annoying <u>at times</u>. I thought that a cat would sleep all day, but my cat

is much more energetic (then) I expected. If he does not go outside to (make)
FROLIC is a verb
frolic) in the backyard, he starts to behave a bit neurotically.
word form
(The) people also say that (the) dogs are more frie(ndlier) than the cats, but I
use possessive form
remember a couple of <u>the dogs of my family</u> that were not friendly at all. Our

Chihuahua was named "Wagster," and he did not like anyone. Every time
word choice
someone rang our doorbell, he would (to) bark (greatly) to scare the visitor away.
word choice - dictionary!
Once he even <u>bit a little</u> at my grandmother! She never thought that the dogs

were friendly after that experience.

Where is the TOPIC SENTENCE?

My friend Aimee had a cat that was so aloof and distant that I never saw it when I came to visit. When I dropped by her house, the cat always hid itself under a bed.

Add drama by adding "No matter how many times," instead of simple "when."

meaning?

Combine?

Connector?

My friend Jasper has a dog that is almost very friendly. It licks and licks and licks until I wish it were not quite so friendly. Jasper does not live in my hometown now, and he probably does not have any pets now.

How is this information relevant to your essay?

How did this stereotypes about the cats and the dogs develop? As with most prejudices, they reflect more about the peoples who express them than about what is true. Both the cats and the dogs make good pets, and they are bad. It all depends on the individual animal.

You can do better than this. Make the 2nd clause parallel to the 1st.

Very good conclusion

Cats vs. Dogs—this is the dilemma that pet owners face. I enjoyed reading your essay, which tries to debunk the stereotypes about these two animals.

Your ideas are expressed relatively clearly, but to improve this essay, you must raise the level of your vocabulary. A good writer avoids bland words such as NICE and GOOD. Use more specific adjectives.

Paragraph 4 needs work.

The conclusion is solid in content but needs better language.

Activity 6   **Revised Essay**

Read the revised version of the essay, now titled "The Truth About Cats and Dogs." What has been changed? What still needs improvement?

Essay 3C   **The Truth About Cats and Dogs**

I used to think that dogs were better than cats as pets. As I was growing up, my family had a lot of dogs—<u>mutts</u>, poodles, Chihuahuas, dachshunds—but we never had cats because my father is allergic to them. I always assumed that when I grew up, I would have a dog as a pet. My life as a pet owner changed one night when a tiny kitten showed up at my door. He was cold, wet, and hungry, and I was afraid he would die on my doorstep if I did not help him. I never saw myself as a cat owner, but now that I am one, I realize that most of the stereotypes about cats and dogs are untrue.

Cats are supposed to be <u>standoffish</u> and uncurious as well as <u>finicky</u> and <u>meticulous</u>. My cat, however, is very friendly and even a little messy. He always wants my attention, which can be annoying at times, especially when I am trying to cook or study. I thought that a cat would sleep all day, but my cat is much more energetic than I expected. If he does not go outside to frolic in the backyard, he starts to behave a bit neurotically. Obviously, my cat does not fit the stereotype of the average cat.

People also say that dogs are friendlier than cats, but I remember a couple of my family's dogs that were not friendly at all. Our Chihuahua was named Wagster, and he did not like anyone. Every time someone rang our doorbell, he would bark <u>ferociously</u> to scare the visitor away. Once he even

<u>nipped</u> at my grandmother! She never thought that all dogs were friendly after that experience. We also had another dog named Rover that used to bark loudly whenever the postal carrier came to deliver our mail. Even though our carrier never met our dog, I am certain that he knew that Rover was not a very friendly dog.

Of course, I have known both cats and dogs that <u>fulfill</u> the stereotypes as well. My friend Aimee had a cat that was so aloof and distant that I never saw it when I came to visit. No matter how many times I dropped by her house, the cat always hid itself under a bed. Likewise, my friend Jasper has a dog that is almost ridiculously friendly. It licks and licks and licks until I wish it were not quite so friendly.

How did these stereotypes about cats and dogs develop? As with most prejudices, they reflect more about the people who express them than about what is true. Both cats and dogs make good pets, and both of them can make bad pets. It all depends on the individual animal, and no one should judge an animal before getting to know it.

mutts: dogs of mixed breed
standoffish: unfriendly, aloof
finicky: very fussy, hard to please
meticulous: extremely careful and precise

ferociously: savagely, fiercely
nipped: grabbed and bit
fulfill: make real

Analyzing Content and Organization

Activity 7   *Analyzing the Content*

Answer these questions about the revised version (3C) of "The Truth About Cats and Dogs."

1. What is the topic of the essay? _____

2. What is the writer's thesis? _____

    _____

3. What are some features of cats that the writer discusses?

    _____

    _____

4. What are some features of dogs that the writer discusses?

    _____

    _____

5. According to the writer, what are common stereotypes about cats?

    _____

    _____

6. Write one detail that supports the thesis statement.

    _____

    _____

7. This essay is organized by (circle one): block method   point-by-point method

WRITER'S NOTE: *Used to* + Verb

You know several ways to express past tense in English:

-ed (want**ed**)   had (**had** gone)   was (**was** eating).

Another way to express an action in the past is with **used to**. We use *used to +
verb* to describe an action that happened in the past many times but is no longer true.

"When I was a child, I **used to** <u>hate</u> onions, but now I eat them on salads
all the time."

Use *used to + verb* as a special way to say that something happened (repeatedly)
in the past but is unlikely to happen again.

Activity 8 | *Analyzing the Organization*

*Read the outline of "The Truth About Cats and Dogs." Then use information in the box to
complete the outline.*

- common stereotypes about dogs

- many stereotypes about cats and dogs are untrue

- the people who express them

- a cat that fulfills feline stereotypes

- an example of a cat that defies these stereotypes

I. Introduction

    A.   Describe my previous beliefs about pets

    B.   Tell what my plans for pet ownership were and how they changed

    C.   Thesis: _____

II. Body Paragraph 1

    A.   Discuss common stereotypes about cats.

    B.   Provide _____

III. Body Paragraph 2

    A.   Discuss _____

    B.   Provide an example of a dog that defies these stereotypes

IV. Body Paragraph 3

    A.   Provide an example of _____

    B.   Provide an example of a dog that fulfills canine stereotypes

V. Conclusion

    A.   Suggest that stereotypes reveal more about _____

_____ than the actual truth.

    B.   Conclude that both cats and dogs make good pets

TRANSITIONS AND CONNECTORS IN COMPARISON-CONTRAST ESSAYS

Transitions and connectors are important in comparison-contrast essays; they help to keep clear the relationship between ideas about the two subjects. This is particularly true in the point-by-point method. In the block method, the subject being discussed is clear because the whole paragraph is about that one subject. However, when the point-by-point method is used, both subjects are discussed with each point. Precise use of transitions helps the reader to follow the writer's comparisons.

These transition words and phrases focus on similarities:

also	compared to	like	similar to
as	have in common	likewise	similarly
as well (as)	in the same way	(the) same as	too
both			

These transition words and phrases focus on differences:

although	even though	on the other hand	unlike
but	however	(the) opposite	whereas
contrary to	in contrast (to)	(the) reverse	while
contrasted with	instead	though	yet
(X) differs (from Y)	on the contrary	unless	

Activity 9   ***Using Transitions and Connectors***

Reread the revised version (3C) of "The Truth About Cats and Dogs" on pages 70-71. Find and list six transitions or connectors and write the paragraph number after each. One has been done for you.

Transitions that show similarity	Transitions that show differences
1. _also_____ (3)	1. _____ ( )
2. _____ ( )	2. _____ ( )
3. _____ ( )	
4. _____ ( )	

VOCABULARY FOR BETTER WRITING

Vocabulary is important in writing. The following activities will help you to improve your knowledge and application of better vocabulary.

Activity 10	*Improving Your Vocabulary*

Circle the word or phrase to the right that is most closely related to the word on the left. The first one has been done for you.

1. mutts   (mixed breeds)   pure breeds

2. allergic   sneezes   breathes

3. assumed   believed   bothered

4. stereotypes   emotions   preconceptions

5. aloof   solitary   friendly

6. distant   alone   together

7. finicky   indulgent   picky

8. meticulous   careful   sloppy

9. annoying   helpful   bothersome

10. frolic   play   study

11. neurotically   kindly   crazily

12. ferociously   viciously   sweetly

13. nipped   bit   drank

14. experience   adventure   mistake

15. standoffish	haughty	friendly
16. uncurious	bored	engaged
17. dropped by	visited	bombed
18. ridiculously	antagonistically	humorously
19. prejudices	biases	hopes
20. individual	sole	friendly

Activity 11 — *Using Collocations*

Fill in the blank with the word on the left that most naturally completes the phrase. The first one has been done for you.

1. what / that   used to think __that_____

2. up / down   growing _____

3. to / of   allergic _____ them

4. up / in   showed _____ at my door

5. about / to   all of the stereotypes _____

6. be / are   supposed to _____

7. at / in   _____ times

8. in / on   to frolic _____ the backyard

9. than / then   dogs are friendlier _____ cats

10. in / at   not friendly _____ all

11. ring / punch   _____ a doorbell

12. around / away   to scare a person _____

13. at / by   dropped _____ her house

14. what / that   to the extent _____

15. at / of   the truth _____ the matter

16. on / about   it all depends _____

GRAMMAR FOR BETTER WRITING

This section contains grammar that might be review for you or it might be new. Grammatical errors in essays distract the reader and get in the way of clear communication. Your goal should be to create error-free essays. This section will help you to become a better editor of your own writing. See Appendix 1, pages 192–201, for additional grammar practice.

Grammar Topic 3.1   Comparative Forms *(-er, more/less; as . . . as, the same . . . as)*

There are two ways to form the comparative form of adjectives and adverbs.

1. If the word is one syllable, add *-er* to the end of the word.

   fast**er**, light**er**

If the word contains two syllables and ends in *-y*, change the *-y* to *-i* and add *-er*.

   heav**ier**, laz**ier**

2. Some words must be preceded by *more* or *less* to form the comparison.

   more comfortable, **less** quickly

To say that two things are similar, we use *as . . . as* with adjectives and *the same . . . as* with nouns.

adjective
↓
The concrete block is **as <u>heavy</u> as** the wood block.

noun
↓
The concrete block has **the same <u>weight</u> as** the wood block.

Activity 12   **Working with Comparative Forms**

Write the correct comparative form of the word in parentheses.

1. (difficult)   Writing a business letter is _____ than composing the

    same message in an e-mail.

2. (reliable)   I decided not to buy a Ford truck. To me, the Ford is _____

    than the Toyota.

3. (expensive)   It did not matter which brand we bought because one is just as

    _____ as the other.

4. (deep)   Studying physics is a _____ and more complex process

    than most people imagine.

5. (concisely)   Most readers prefer the short news clips on Channel 9. It would be impossible

    to present the news _____ than those newscasters do.

6. (lucky)   In the very first lines of the poem, we learn that the main character's jealousy

    can be attributed to the fact that her younger sister is so much

    _____ than she is.

Grammar Topic 3.2   **Parallel Comparison**

When writers create sentences that contain pairs or a series of items, parallel construction in comparison is important. A parallel comparison means that the writer is comparing a noun with a noun or a clause with a clause.

Incorrect: In general, **a dog's tongue** is longer than **a cat**.

This is wrong because it compares a body part with another animal.

Correction 1: In general, **a dog's tongue** is longer than **a cat's tongue**.

Correction 2: In general, **a dog's tongue** is longer than **a cat's**.

| Grammar Topic 3.2 | Parallel Comparison (continued) |

Incorrect: The **smell of fried chicken** is not as strong as **fried fish**.

This is wrong because it compares a smell with a food.

Correction 1:   The **smell of fried chicken** is not as strong as the **smell of fried fish**.

Correction 2:   **Fried chicken** does not smell as strong as **fried fish**.

Note: To avoid using the same noun twice, it is common to use the pronouns *that* (singular) or *those* (plural).

In some countries, the **cost** of water is higher than the **cost** of oil.

Better: In some countries, the **cost** of water is higher than **that** of oil.

Activity 13   *Working with Parallel Comparisons*

Each sentence contains an error in parallel comparison. Circle the two items that are being incorrectly compared. Then rewrite the sentence correctly, according to Grammar Topic 3.2. The first one has been done for you.

1. According to the most recent data, the (population of Spain) is larger than (Greece)

    <u>According to the most recent data, the population of Spain is larger than the</u>

    <u>population of Greece.</u>

    <u>According to the most recent data, the population of Spain is larger than that of Greece.</u>

2. The company report indicates that January had more sales than the sales in February.

    _____

    _____

    _____

3. With only five days until the deadline, our team's project is not as good as the other team.

_____

_____

_____

4. In theory, both classes are equally good. However, last Monday produced a clearly different picture. Professor Smith's students scored better than Professor Beiler.

_____

_____

_____

Grammar Topic 3.3				Non-Count Nouns

A non-count noun cannot be counted.

food:	butter	sugar	salt	pepper	soup
liquid:	milk	coffee	water	juice	cream
subjects:	English	math	science	music	biology
abstract:	love	honesty	poverty	crime	advice

Note: Count nouns can be counted: *three <u>dogs</u>, two <u>computers</u>, one <u>house</u>, ten <u>motorcycles</u>.*

Activity 14   *Working with Count and Non-Count Nouns*

Write many *in front of count nouns and make them plural. Write* much *in front of non-count nouns. (They have no plural form.)*

1. _____ pain

2. _____ information

3. _____ decision

4. _____ money

5. _____ pill

6. _____ homework

7. _____ cooperation

8. _____ requirement

Grammar Topic 3.4	Confusing Words: *than / then*

The words *than* and *then* sound alike, but they are used very differently. Do not confuse them in your writing.

then = adverb (time)	We are planning to return these books to the library. **Then** we are going to the bank.
than = conjunction	China has more people **than** Brazil does.
= preposition	China has more people **than** cars.

Activity 15   **Working with Confusing Words: than / then**

Complete each sentence with than *or* then.

1. If more _____ fifty people come to the meeting, we will need

   to have it in a larger room.

2. Most supermarkets have express lanes for customers who are purchasing fewer

   _____ ten items.

3. The rain finally stopped. _____ the players came out onto the

   field again.

4. If you receive an increase in your salary, _____ you can buy

   that new furniture.

5. The 1960s were difficult years for the United States. Many Americans thought

   the country might suffer a nuclear disaster _____; fortunately,

   history proved them wrong.

Grammar Topic 3.5   Word-Parts Practice

You can increase your vocabulary in two basic ways. One is to learn words that you have never seen before. The second is to learn word parts, which will help you to understand how other words are constructed. Recognizing word parts and using them correctly will increase your vocabulary and thus improve your writing.

Activity 16   *Editing Word Parts*

Read the paragraph. Five of the eight underlined words contain an error with word parts. Correct the error or write C (correct). If you need more information about word parts, review Appendix 3, pages 218-220. The first one has been done for you.

A young man was worried because his grandmother was sad, and he wondered what he could do to cheer her up. He lived far away, so he could not be there to keep her company. He decided to send her a **❶** special _____C_____ gift—a parrot that could talk to her so that she would not feel so **❷** loneliness _____.

When he went to the pet store, he was **❸** surprising _____ to find a parrot that could speak not one but six languages! This special parrot was **❹** outrageous _____ expensive, but the young man decided that it was worth this extra cost to buy such a wonderful gift for his grandmother. He bought the parrot and sent it to his grandmother's house.

A week later, he called her to see how she and the parrot were **❺** getting _____ along. "Grandmother," he asked, "how did you like my gift?" The grandmother replied, "Well, the parrot was good, but it was a little tough. I should have **❻** cooked _____ it more." **❼** Shocking _____ beyond belief, the man replied, "What? You ate a parrot that could speak six languages?" The grandmother **❽** quick _____ said, "Well, if the parrot could speak six languages, why didn't it say anything before I put it in the microwave?"

Activity 17   *Review of Grammar Topics 3.1–3.5*

Seven of the following ten sentences contain an error involving one of the grammar topics featured in this unit. Write C before the three correct sentences. Write X before the incorrect sentences, circle the error, and write a correction above it.

_____ 1. If this machine could produce more item, our company would buy many more of these machines than we are currently purchasing.

_____ 2. Since the orange juice at this restaurant is more fresher than at the one across the street, I want to eat here.

_____ 3. It is so much more comfortable to spend an evening at home then to go out at night.

_____ 4. My friend Mark took a trip to Las Vegas, which he thinks is more fun than a trip to Los Angeles.

_____ 5. The Pittsburgh Steelers' quarterback is faster than the Philadelphia Eagles.

_____ 6. Did you get two butters at the store, as I requested?

_____ 7. I love my new car; it is more fast and sporty than my last one.

_____ 8. Camping can be a lot of fun, but all of the insects can really annoy me.

_____ 9. There is certainly great poverties in this city.

_____ 10. It is always a great idea to save some of your money for a rainy day, but a lot of people find it difficult not to spend their money immediately.

Activity 18   *Editing a Paragraph: Review of Grammar Topics 3.1–3.5*

Seven of the ten underlined words in this paragraph contain an error involving one of the grammar topics featured in this unit. Correct the errors on the lines provided. If the word or phrase is correct, write C.

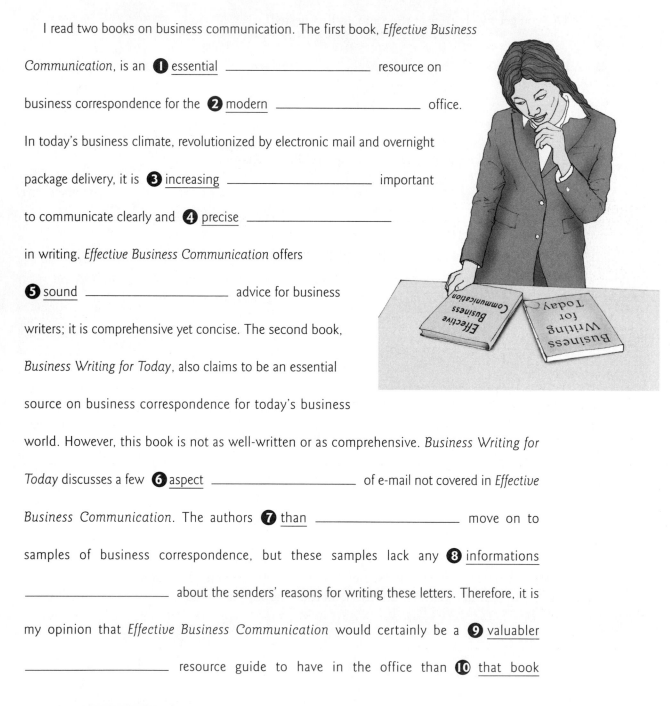

I read two books on business communication. The first book, *Effective Business Communication*, is an ❶ essential _____ resource on business correspondence for the ❷ modern _____ office.

In today's business climate, revolutionized by electronic mail and overnight package delivery, it is ❸ increasing _____ important to communicate clearly and ❹ precise _____ in writing. *Effective Business Communication* offers ❺ sound _____ advice for business writers; it is comprehensive yet concise. The second book, *Business Writing for Today*, also claims to be an essential source on business correspondence for today's business world. However, this book is not as well-written or as comprehensive. *Business Writing for Today* discusses a few ❻ aspect _____ of e-mail not covered in *Effective Business Communication*. The authors ❼ than _____ move on to samples of business correspondence, but these samples lack any ❽ informations _____ about the senders' reasons for writing these letters. Therefore, it is my opinion that *Effective Business Communication* would certainly be a ❾ valuabler _____ resource guide to have in the office than ❿ that book _____.

STUDENT ESSAY WRITING

In this section, you will go through the seven steps in writing a five-paragraph essay. To review the details of each step, see Unit 1, pages 8–15.

| Activity 19 | *Original Comparison-Contrast Essay* |

Using the seven steps below, write a five-paragraph comparison-contrast essay. Your teacher may assign a topic, you may think of one yourself, or you may choose from the suggestions in Step 1. You might need to do research.

Step 1: Choosing a Topic

For a comparison-contrast essay, you want to choose a topic for which you can develop three solid points comparing or contrasting the two sides.

Suggestions:

Humanities:	Comparison-contrast essays are quite common in the humanities. If you are a literature major, you might write an essay comparing how two different authors address a similar theme. History majors might compare the ways in which two different leaders responded to similar historical moments. Political science majors might compare the relative merits of two systems of government.
Sciences:	Describe a scientific experiment that you performed in which you compared and contrasted two processes. What did you learn from these experiments?
Business:	Think of the last major purchase you made (or a major purchase that you will soon make), such as a television, stereo, car, or condominium. How did you make your decision? Describe how you compared and contrasted your options. Develop a thesis that reveals how you finally made your decision.
Personal:	Who are the two people you most admire? Write an essay describing the influence that these two people have had on your life. You do not have to argue that one was more important than the other.

1. What topic did you choose? _____

2. Why did you choose this topic? _____

_____

Step 2: Brainstorming

Use this space to jot down as many ideas about the topic as you can.

Brainstorming Box

Step 3: Outlining

Prepare a simple outline of your essay. (This outline is a point-by-point outline, but you may use the block comparison if your teacher approves.)

Title: _____

I. Introduction _____

_____

Background information _____

_____

Thesis statement: _____

_____

II. Point 1

_____

_____

III. Point 2

_____

_____

IV. Point 3

_____

_____

V. Conclusion _____

_____

Peer Editing of Outlines

Give your outline to a partner. This space is for your partner to write comments about your outline.

1. Is there anything in the outline that looks unclear to you?

   _____

   _____

   _____

2. Can you think of an area in the outline that needs more development? Do you have any specific suggestions?

   _____

   _____

   _____

3. If you have any other ideas or suggestions, write them here.

_____

_____

_____

Step 4: Writing the First Draft

Use the information from Steps 1–3 to write the first draft of your five-paragraph comparison-contrast essay.

Step 5: Peer Editing

Exchange essays with someone else. Read that person's essay and offer feedback on Peer Editing Sheet 3, pages 239–240.

Step 6: Revising Your Draft

Read the comments on Peer Editing Sheet 3 about your essay. Then reread your essay. Can you identify places where you plan to revise? List what you are going to do.

1. _____

_____

_____

2. _____

_____

_____

3. _____

_____

_____

Use all the information from the previous activities to write the final version of your paper. Writers will often need to write a third or even a fourth draft to express their ideas clearly. Write as many drafts as necessary to produce a good essay.

Step 7: Proofing the Final Paper

Be sure to proofread your paper several times before you submit it.

TOPICS FOR WRITING

Here are ten topics for additional comparison-constrast essay writing.

TOPIC 1 → Compare and/or contrast two videogame systems such as Playstation and Gamecube. Which videogame system is better and why?

TOPIC 2 → Of the two most recent Oscar-winning "Best Picture" winners, which do you like better? Why?

TOPIC 3 → Compare and/or contrast two of your favorite restaurants.

TOPIC 4 → If you were making a movie of your favorite book, who would you cast in the lead role? Compare and/or contrast two actors/actresses and discuss which would be the more appropriate choice.

TOPIC 5 → How did you decide to attend the school you are now attending? Describe the compare and/or contrast process you used in deciding to attend your current school.

TOPIC 6 → Compare and/or contrast the teaching styles of two of your teachers. Which teaching style is more effective? Why?

TOPIC 7 → Compare and/or contrast your hometown to the city you live in now. Which one would you prefer to live in if you had your choice? Why?

TOPIC 8 → Compare and/or contrast your favorite vacation destinations. If you could return to only one for the rest of your life, which would it be? Why?

TOPIC 9 → Look at a local ballot measure in an upcoming election and compare and/or contrast the opposing sides. (Alternatively, you could write about an imaginary election situation.) How would you vote and why?

TOPIC 10 → Compare and/or contrast two sports teams. Which do you think will win the national championship this year? Why?

Online Study Center For additional activities, go to the *Greater Essays* Online Study Center at http://esl.college.hmco.com/pic/greateressays1e

Cause-Effect Essays

Writing Goal:	To learn how to write a cause/effect essay
Grammar Topic 4.1:	Maintaining Consistent Pronouns
Grammar Topic 4.2:	Sentence Fragments
Grammar Topic 4.3:	Consistent Verb Tense
Grammar Topic 4.4:	Confusing Words: *it's / its*
Grammar Topic 4.5:	Word Parts Practice

WHAT IS A CAUSE-EFFECT ESSAY?

We all understand cause-effect relationships. For example, if you stay up late the night before a test, hanging out with friends and not studying, you will likely not perform as well as possible on a test the following day. A cause-effect essay tells how one event (the cause) leads to another event (the effect).

Typically, cause-effect essays work in one of two ways:

- They analyze the ways in which several effects result from a particular cause. ("Focus-on-Effects" Method)

- They analyze the ways in which several causes lead to a particular effect. ("Focus-on-Causes" Method)

Either approach is an effective means of discussing the possible relationship between the two events.

In cause-effect essays, it is easy to suggest that because one event preceded another event, the former event caused the latter. Simply because one event follows another event sequentially does not mean that the two actions are related. For example, people often complain that as soon as they finish washing their car, it starts to rain. Obviously, washing a car does not cause rain. Writers need to be sure that the cause-effect relationship they describe is logical.

HOW IS A CAUSE-EFFECT ESSAY ORGANIZED?

There are two basic ways to organize a cause-effect essay: **focus-on-effects** or **focus-on-causes**.

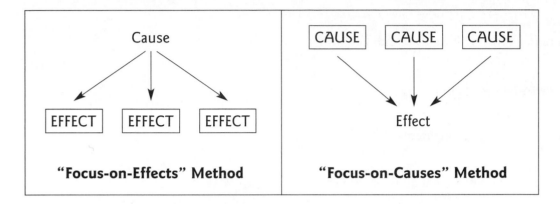

If your assignment is to write a cause-effect essay on the topic of World War II, you could write two kinds of essays:

- In a focus-on-effects essay, you would write about things that happened as a result of the war. For example, large parts of Europe were completely destroyed, and many people died from starvation.

- In a focus-on-causes essay, you would write about things that happened before the war that led to the start of the war.

TOPICS FOR CAUSE-EFFECT ESSAYS

What is a good topic for a cause-effect essay? This type of essay may focus more on the cause or on the effect, but most writers answer this question by thinking of an effect or a final result. The brainstorming stage then includes thinking about one or more causes of that effect.

Here are some possible effects (or results). What might be some causes for each of these effects?

- Pollution is a problem in my state.

- A large percentage of adults cannot read well.

- The rate of violent crime has dropped.

Activity 1

Identifying Topics for Cause-Effect Essays

Read these eight topics. Put a check (✓) next to the four that could be good topics for cause-effect essays.

_____ 1. the reasons that a particular candidate won an election

_____ 2. Germany versus Spain as a vacation destination

_____ 3. a trip to visit my grandparents

_____ 4. the increasing use of computers in schools

_____ 5. outlining dietary guidelines for children

_____ 6. how to play the piano

_____ 7. why a student received a scholarship

_____ 8. why the birth rate is falling in Italy

Can you think of two additional topics that would be excellent for a cause-effect essay?

9. _____

10. _____

Topic Details

After you have selected a topic, your task is to determine whether you will focus more on the causes of the issue or the effects of the issue. This process will also help you to select and develop supporting details for your essay.

Activity 2   **Brainstorming for Two Methods**

One of the topics that we hear so much about in today's society is stress. In this activity, you will use the space in the boxes to brainstorm ideas for an essay on the topic of stress. In the first box, your organization will address the focus-on-effects method. In the second box, the method of organization will address the focus-on-causes. Work with other students and/or discuss your answers with other students after you complete these tasks.

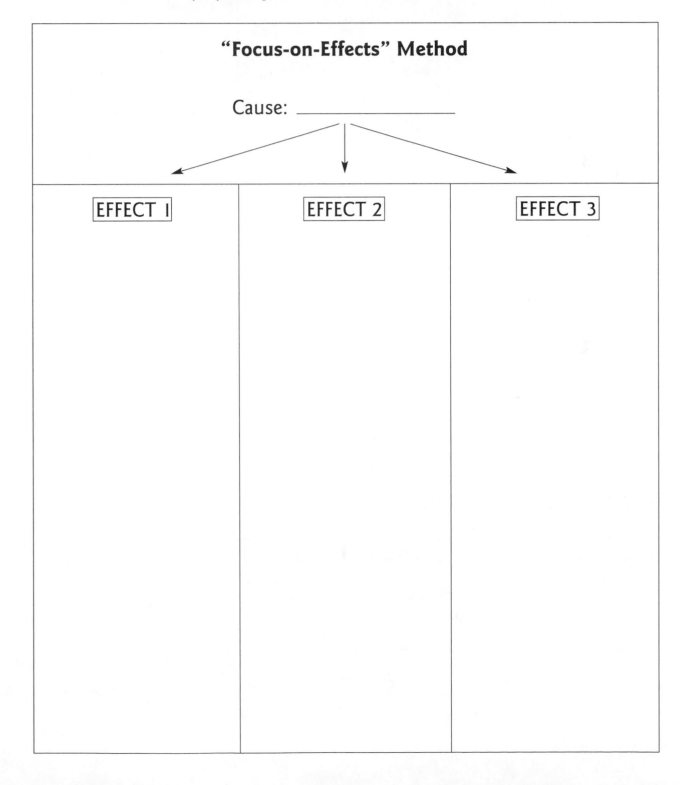

"Focus-on-Effects" Method

Cause: _____

EFFECT 1	EFFECT 2	EFFECT 3

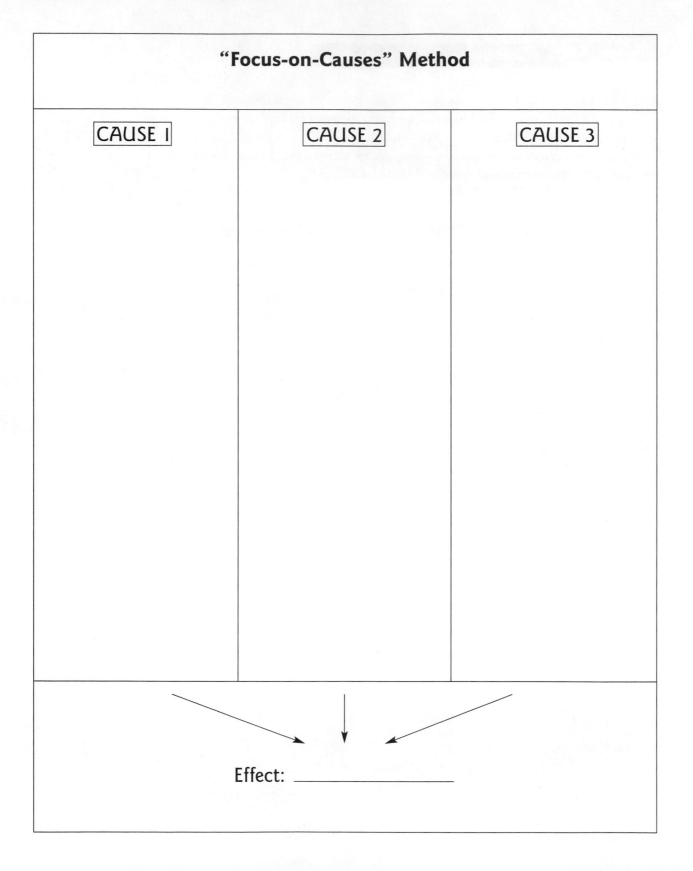

STUDYING A SAMPLE CAUSE-EFFECT ESSAY

In this section, you will study three versions of a five-paragraph cause-effect essay: a rough draft, the same rough draft with teacher comments, and the revised essay.

Activity 3	*Warming Up to the Topic*

Answer these questions individually. Then discuss them with a partner or in a small group

1. How often do you listen to music in a week? _____ Do you usually listen to music on the radio or to music that you have bought? _____ How many CDs (or tapes or albums) do you own? _____

2. Have you ever made a copy of a music CD? _____ Many people download music from the Internet illegally. Have you ever done this? _____

3. Some people believe that because so many people are downloading music from the Internet, music companies will eventually go bankrupt. Do you think this will happen? _____ Why or why not? _____

   _____

4. Although copying music is illegal, many people continue to download copyrighted materials from the Internet. What are some of the reasons that have caused this practice to be so prevalent?

   _____

   _____

   _____

   _____

   _____

   _____

Activity 4   **First Draft of the Essay**

As you read this rough draft, look for areas that need improvement.

Essay 4A   Music, Computers, and the Recording Industry

The recording industry is in a big hole. Albums and CDs are not selling as much as several years ago, and this <u>trend</u> shows no sign of reversing. For the industry as a whole, profits are down ten percent inside the last three year. What has caused this downward <u>spiral</u> for the music industry? The answer is an equipment with which I am writing this essay: the personal computer. There are three reasons that the computer has had a bad effect in the recording industry.

Due to it is popular to share computer sound files, consumers no longer feel that they are need to purchase music. Many people think it is <u>morally</u> acceptable—not to mention convenience—to download music files for free via file-sharing services. A couple of mouse-button click, and <u>presto</u>! Now you "own" on your own computer that nice little tune that you have been <u>humming</u>. Then it was just a couple of more clicks until it was burned on a CD for you. With this level of convenience, it was easy to see why record companies are <u>feeling the pinch</u>.

Computers allow music people to <u>market</u> and sell their own music. Music people can record and create their own CDs at a relatively <u>modest</u> cost these days. Before the development of the personal computer, this would have been impossibility. For this reason, it makes less sense for music people to give away a part of their profits to a record company for activities that he can accomplish themselves.

The recording industry bears some of the blame for its own problems. Simply because they have been shy about using personal computers to sell its products. It has long annoy me that record companies primarily sell albums when all I want is one song. Too many albums contained only one good song, and I do not like to spend money for an entire album when I wanted only one song. The recording industry should package and sell music in a way that consumers want. And take advantage of personal computers to market songs to individual consumers.

If the downward trends in the recording industry continues, there will still be a recording industry? It is quite possible that the recording industry will stop over time if it becomes no longer profitable for them to market and sell music. Performing artists have to advertise themselves through smaller <u>venues</u>, and consumers might need to seek out new music if its no longer marketed directly to us. The computer will <u>bring about</u> tremendous changes to the recording industry. The industry will have to move quickly to <u>retain</u> its <u>relevance</u> in the today's economy.

---

trend: a new style that people follow

spiral: a winding curve that moves toward a fixed center

morally: honorably, ethically

presto: an expression that indicates something has been accomplished instantly

humming: singing without words

feeling the pinch: suffering the consequences

market: sell or offer something for sale

modest: moderate in amount

venues: locations

bring about: cause to happen

retain: keep possession of something

relevance: having an important relationship to the matter being considered

Activity 5   **Teacher Comments on First Draft**

Read the teacher comments on the first draft of "Music, Computers, and the Recording Industry." Are these the same things that you noticed?

Your title is not very catchy, but it works OK.

Essay 4B   Music, Computers, and the Recording Industry

vague vocab

The recording industry is in a (big hole) Albums and CDs are not selling

they were (You need parallel comparison.)

as much as several years ago, and this trend shows no sign of reversing. For

word choice

the industry as a whole, profits are down ten percent <u>inside</u> the last three

yea(r) What has caused this downward spiral for the music industry? The

non-count noun

answer is <u>an equipment</u> with which I am writing this essay: the personal

prep.

computer. There are three reasons that the computer has had a (bad) effect (in)

the recording industry.

word choice: BAD is a beginning word. How about DELETERIOUS?

"Due to" is followed by a noun, not a sentence

Due to (it is popular to share) computer sound files, consumers no longer

feel that they (are need) to purchase music. Many people think it is morally

?

acceptable—not to mention <u>convenien(ce)</u>—to download music files for free

via file-sharing services. A couple of mouse-button click(s) and presto! Now

use a more specific word

you "own" on your own computer that (nice) little tune that you have been

humming. Then it (was) just a couple of more clicks until it (was) burned on a

CD for you. With this level of convenience, it (was) easy to see why record

Why change to past tense?

companies are feeling the pinch.

Transition?   *vocab?*

Computers allow <u>music people</u> to market and sell their own music.

Music people can record and create their own CDs at a relatively modest cost

these days. Before the development of the personal computer, this would

word form

have been <u>impossibility</u>. For this reason, it makes less sense for music people to give away a part of their profits to a record company for activities that he

can accomplish themselves.

Pronouns: be consistent with singular & plural

Transition?

The recording industry bears some of the blame for its own problems.

wrong word - people are shy, not companies - What do you mean?

Simply because they have been shy about using personal computers to sell its

products. It has long annoy me that record companies primarily sell albums

verb form   *good adverb*   *fragment*

when all I want is one song. Too many albums contained only one good song,

Why change to past tense?

and I do not like to spend money for an entire album when I wanted only one

song. The recording industry should package and sell music in a way that

consumers want. And take advantage of personal computers to market songs

to individual consumers. *fragment*

If the downward trends in the recording industry continues, there will

still be a recording industry? It is quite possible that the recording industry

word choice: die?

will stop over time if it becomes no longer profitable for them to market and

sell music. Performing artists have to advertise themselves through smaller

Parallel? Repeat modal "might"   *word form*

venues, and consumers might need to seek out new music if its no longer

Pronoun?

marketed directly to us. The computer will bring about tremendous changes

connect   *here, future is correct*

to the recording industry. The industry will have to move quickly to retain its

relevance in the today's economy.

excellent word combinations!

Your ideas flow really well in this essay. I sense that you feel strongly about this issue.

I especially liked your vocabulary choices in the last paragraph.

Paragraphs 3 and 4 need transitions. Do you see that your opening sentences sound rather abrupt?

Activity 6   **Revised Essay**

Read the revised version of the essay, now titled "Modern Music Technology: Downloading or Stealing?" What has been changed? What still needs improvement?

Essay 4C   Modern Music Technology: Downloading or Stealing?

The recording industry is in a <u>slump</u>. Albums and CDs are not selling as much as they were several years ago, and this trend shows no sign of reversing. For the industry as a whole, profits are down ten percent within the last three years. What has caused this downward spiral for the music industry? The answer is the same piece of equipment with which I am writing this essay: the personal computer. There are three reasons that the computer has had a <u>deleterious</u> effect on the recording industry.

Because of the popularity of sharing computer sound files, consumers no longer feel that they need to purchase music. Many people think it is morally acceptable—not to mention convenient—to download music files for free via file-sharing services. A couple of mouse-button clicks, and presto! Now you "own" on your own computer that <u>catchy</u> little tune that you have been humming. Then it is just a couple of more clicks until it is burned on a CD for you. With this level of convenience, it is easy to see why record companies are feeling the pinch.

In addition, computers allow musicians to market and sell their own music. Musicians can record and create their own CDs at a relatively modest cost these days. Before the development of the personal computer, most musicians could not afford to record their own music, but now the costs are much more reasonable. For this reason, it makes less sense for musicians to give away a part of their profits to a record company for activities that they can accomplish themselves.

Furthermore, the recording industry bears some of the blame for its own problems simply because it has been <u>recalcitrant</u> about using personal computers to sell its products. It has long annoyed me that record companies primarily sell whole albums when only one of the songs is of interest to me. I do not like to waste my money on an entire album and then find out that the album has just one good song on it. The recording industry should package and sell music in a way that consumers want and take advantage of personal computers to market songs to individual consumers.

If the downward trends in the recording industry continue, will there still be a recording industry? It is quite possible that the recording industry will die over time if it becomes no longer profitable to market and sell music. Performing artists might have to advertise themselves through smaller venues, and consumers might need to seek out new music if it is no longer marketed directly to them. The computer has brought about tremendous changes to the recording industry, and the industry will have to move quickly to retain its relevance in today's economy.

slump: a sudden decline
deleterious: harmful
catchy: attractive or appealing
recalcitrant: not willing, stubborn

Analyzing Content and Organization

Activity 7   *Analyzing the Content*

Answer these questions about the revised version (4C) of "Modern Music Technology: Downloading or Stealing?"

1. What is the topic? _____

2. Write the thesis statement here: _____

_____

3. What is the effect that the writer describes in the essay?

_____

_____

4. What are some of the causes that the writer describes?

_____

_____

5. Is the writer's reasoning convincing? _____

   How could it be improved? _____

_____

Activity 8   *Analyzing the Organization*

Read the outline of "Modern Music Technology: Downloading or Stealing?" Then use information in the box to complete the outline.

- a decrease in sales of CDs and albums   - personal computer

- current conditions   - musicians

- the recording industry

I. Introduction

    A.   Describe the current troubled situation of the recording industry

    B.   Thesis: The _____ has caused many of the recording

           industry's woes

II. Body Paragraph 1:   Show that the popularity of sharing computer files has led to _____

_____

III. Body Paragraph 2:   Describe how computers allow _____ to market

           their own music without the recording industry

IV. Body Paragraph 3:   Suggest that _____ bears some responsibility

           because it has not marketed through personal computers

V. Conclusion

    A.   Ponder the future of the recording industry if _____ remain

    B.   Suggest that the recording industry must act quickly to reverse these declines

WRITER'S NOTE: Language for Conversation and for Writing

Language in conversation, especially with people you know, is usually informal. Language in writing, in contrast, is often more formal. Language in writing has a different style than language in conversation. We use different vocabulary and sometimes different structures for conversation and for writing.

Here are some examples of differences in these two language styles.

Conversation	Writing
kids	children
a cool movie	a great movie, a really interesting movie
See you later!	I hope to see you soon.
Well, this is what . . .	This is what . . .

TRANSITIONS AND CONNECTORS IN CAUSE-EFFECT ESSAYS

The most commonly used transitions and connectors in cause-effect essays are words or phrases that indicate causation or effect. Perhaps the most familiar cause-effect transition word is *because*: "X happened *because* Y happened."

(X can be) attributed to (Y)	(the) effect (of X)	(X is the) reason for (Y)
because	(a key) factor of (X)	(X is a) reflection of (Y)
because of	furthermore	(as a) result
(X is the) cause of (Y)	if (X), then (Y)	(X) resulted in (Y)
(X is) caused by (Y)	in addition (to)	since
(as a) consequence	(X) leads to (Y)	so
(one) consequence of this (is that . . .)	on account of	therefore
consequently	owing to	this means that . . .
due to	(for this) reason	thus

Activity 9   *Using Transitions and Connectors*

*Reread the revised version (4C) of "Modern Music Technology: Downloading or Stealing?"
on pages 102–103. Find and list six transitions or connectors and write the paragraph number
after each. One has been done for you.*

1. _caused_____ (1)

2. _____ (   )

3. _____ (   )

4. _____ (   )

5. _____ (   )

6. _____ (   )

VOCABULARY FOR BETTER WRITING

Vocabulary is important in writing. The following activities will help you to improve your knowledge and application of better vocabulary.

Activity 10 — *Improving Your Vocabulary*

Circle the word or phrase to the right that is most closely related to the word on the left. The first one has been done for you.

1.	hum	(a song)	a file
2.	slump	frenzy	doldrums
3.	trend	moderate	pattern
4.	reversing	going backward	going forward
5.	profits	more money	less money
6.	spiral	twists and turns	a straight road
7.	deleterious	positive	negative
8.	morally	good behavior	crime
9.	convenient	difficult	easy
10.	via	about	through
11.	presto	immediately	after a long effort
12.	feeling the pinch	in a bind	free to go
13.	to market	to sell	to reverse
14.	modest	reasonable	exorbitant

15. impossible	likely	unlikely
16. activities	decisions	events
17. recalcitrant	anxious	stubborn
18. package	wrap up	argue with
19. advantage	upper hand	handicap
20. industry	natural resources	business
21. advertise	commercial	book
22. tremendous	little	big
23. retain	keep	fly free
24. relevance	importance	unimportance

Activity 11   *Using Collocations*

Fill in the blank with the word on the left that most naturally completes the phrase. The first one has been done for you.

1. in / on   mired _____ in _____ a slump

2. future / ago   several years _____

3. in / of   no sign _____ reversing

4. on / as   _____ a whole

5. within / ago   _____ the last three years

6. about / on   had an effect _____ the economy

7. of / about   due to the popularity _____

8. at / to   they need _____ purchase

9. via / around   to get data _____ file-sharing services

10. on / in   have a program _____ your computer

11. of / in   a couple _____ more clicks

12. at / from   _____ a relatively modest cost

13. away / from   to give _____ a part

14. of / on   bears some _____ the blame

15. about / on   to be recalcitrant _____

16. in / of   its relevance _____ today's economy

17. of / around   so much _____ our money

18. about / over   will die _____ time

19. up / out   to seek _____

20. to / with   if it is no longer marketed directly _____

                    the public

GRAMMAR FOR BETTER WRITING

This section contains grammar that might be review for you or might be new. Grammatical errors in essays distract the reader and get in the way of clear communication. Your goal should be to create error-free essays. This section will help you to become a better editor of your own writing.

Grammar Topic 4.1	Maintaining Consistent Pronouns

Good writers consistently use pronouns of the first, second, or third person throughout an essay: first person (*I / we*), second person (*you*), or third person (*he / she / they*).

Incorrect: When **students** have a major exam, **you** should begin preparing early.

Correct: When **students** have a major exam, **they** should begin preparing early.

Incorrect: In the story, **you** can see that the young girl is going to be successful. **We** know this because of her determination and cleverness.

Correct: In the story, **we** can see that the young girl is going to be successful. **We** know this because of her determination and cleverness.

Activity 12	*Working with Pronoun Consistency*

Make the pronouns consistent in each sentence.

1. It was raining. You could see people running for cover under trees, under awnings, under anything that offers protection. We thought the rain would stop soon.

2. If one studies, you will do well on the quizzes.

3. In Alice Walker's *The Color Purple*, we find it difficult to trust certain characters. You cannot easily explain why, but we have that reaction to them.

4. If I consider her last short story, then we can definitely say that this writer's attitude toward immigration is changing.

Grammar Topic 4.2	**Sentence Fragments**

For many writers, sentence fragments, or incomplete sentences, are difficult to avoid. Because fragments are one of the most serious errors, it is imperative to learn how to recognize and correct them.

Fragment:	I scored 97 on the quiz. **Because I read and studied the textbook often.**
Correction:	I scored 97 on the quiz **because I read and studied the textbook often.**
Fragment:	The postcard was filled with natural beauty. **The red of the sunset, the brilliance of the sand, and the sparkle in the water.**
Correction:	The postcard was filled with natural beauty, **such as the red of the sunset, the brilliance of the sand, and the sparkle in the water.**

For more work with fragments and sentence variety, see Appendix 4, pages 221–230.

Activity 13   *Working with Fragments*

Write C on the line next to complete sentences. Write F if there is a fragment and circle the fragment.

_____ 1. Despite the heavy wind and the torrential rain, the young trees around

the lake were able to survive the bad weather. It was a miracle.

_____ 2. The huge, two-story houses all have a very similar design. With no

difference except the color of the roofs.

_____ 3. The Hudson Valley area of New York State has a rich and colorful

history. One with many ghost stories.

_____ 4. Shopping malls are a very popular tourist attraction in many cities, but

some tourists are not interested in them. Shopping is not for everyone.

_____ 5. Because of the popularity of the film. Producers were anxious to begin

work on its sequel.

_____ 6. The chef added so much spice to the stew that only the most daring of his

patrons tasted it. The result was that less than half of the food was consumed.

_____ 7. There was a strange tension in the air. After so many years of separation.

_____ 8. My mother is so organized that she uses a color-coding system in her

kitchen pantry. My father, on the other hand, is one of the most

unorganized people that I know.

_____ 9. What is a dream and why do we dream? Scientists really do not

understand dreams, but I wish someone could explain them to me.

_____ 10. Thousands of commuters were late for work this morning. Since the bus

workers are on strike over pay and health benefits.

Grammar Topic 4.3   Consistent Verb Tense

Good writers are careful to use the same verb tense throughout an essay. If you are writing about an event in the past tense, keep all the verbs in the past tense. Likewise, if you are describing an event in the present tense, maintain the present tense throughout. Do not change verb tenses without a specific reason.

Activity 14   *Working with Consistent Verb Tense*

Circle the verbs where the tense shifts for no reason.

A good presentation can have significant and long-lasting effects on an audience. What happens between speakers and their presentation and the audience involved many factors. Like any tool, a presentation can be applied with skill to achieve a useful purpose, or it can be used to damage and destroy. Although a hammer was used to build a home, it also can be used to punch holes in a wall. One unethical presentation can affect the way that an audience sees you in all future encounters. Thus, we believed that a good speaker must ask and answer important ethical questions at every point in the speech-making process. Ethical decision making was more than a means of improving speaker credibility; it will remain a moral obligation of every good speaker.

Grammar Topic 4.4   Confusing Words: *it's / its*

The words *its* and *it's* sound alike, but they are used very differently. Do not confuse them in your writing.

it's = contraction (*it is*)   Are you sure that **it's** really after midnight?

its = possessive adjective   The cat will clean **its** fur before going to sleep.

Note 1: A common error is to use *its'* with an apostrophe at the end. Remember that *its'* is not a word.

Note 2: Contractions are used primarily in informal writing such as e-mails and dialogues.

Activity 15   *Working with Confusing Words: it's / its*

Complete each sentence with its *or* it's.

1. IBM released _____ report on Tuesday; _____ full of very

   good economic indicators.

2. The dog howled when I accidentally stepped on _____ tail.

3. Whose key chain is this? If _____ Susan's, then I will call her to tell

   her that _____ here. If _____ Will's, I cannot let him know

   that _____ here because I do not have his cell phone or his home

   number. I would look up his home number in the phone directory, but I believe

   _____ unlisted.

4. Sometimes a dog's bark is worse than _____ bite; this fact is the basis

   for a common proverb.

Grammar Topic 4.5	Word Parts Practice

You can increase your vocabulary in two basic ways. One is to learn words that you have never seen before. The second is to learn word parts, which will help you to understand how other words are constructed. Recognizing word parts and using them correctly will increase your vocabulary and thus improve your writing.

Republicans   ## Democrats

Activity 16   *Editing Word Parts*

Read the following paragraph. Five of the eight underlined words contain an error with word parts. Correct the error or write C (correct). If you need more information about words parts, review Appendix 3, pages 218–220. The first one has been done for you.

In every ❶ president _____ *presidential* _____ election since 1952, voters across the

nation have been asked, "❷ General _____ speaking, do you think of

yourself as a Republican, a Democrat, an ❸ Independent _____, or

what?" Most voters think of themselves as either Republicans or Democrats, but the

❹ proportion _____ of those who think of themselves as

Independents has increased over time. The size of the Democratic Party's ❺ major

_____ has also shrunk. Nevertheless, most ❻ America

_____ today still ❼ identification _____ with

one of these two major parties, and Democrats still outnumber Republicans. The question on

many ❽ political _____ minds is whether this situation will continue

or not.

Activity 17

Review of Grammar Topics 4.1–4.5

Seven of the following ten sentences contain an error involving one of the grammar topics featured in this unit. Write C before the three correct sentences. Write X before the incorrect sentences, circle the error, and write a correction above it.

_____ 1. When the schoolchildren visited the museum, their teacher advised him

to be quiet.

_____ 2. I cannot wait to go to work today. Because I think I am going to get a raise!

_____ 3. Carol Anne played softball when she was younger, and she always hits

home runs then.

_____ 4. It's good for them to have an extra turn, but is it good for us?

_____ 5. Its not healthy to eat only foods with a lot of sugar.

_____ 6. The marching band, entering with a great roar of music.

_____ 7. Simon argued that the judge was incompetent in the trial and that a

mistrial should be declared.

_____ 8. The car needs a new paint job since it's trunk is getting rusty.

_____ 9. Akio knew the truth, but she was afraid to tell the police.

_____ 10. Due to the large influx of immigrants into Canada in the two decades

after World War II.

Activity 18

Editing a Paragraph: Review of Grammar Topics 4.1–4.5

Seven of the ten underlined words in the following paragraph contain an error involving one of the grammar topics featured in this unit. Correct the errors on the lines provided. If the word or phrase is correct, write C.

❶ On _____ e-mail (electronic mail), messages are composed,

transmitted, and usually read on computer ❷ screens. Today _____

e-mail has replaced the ❸ telephone. As _____ the preferred medium to

communicate in business. In 1997, for the first time ever, more e-mail was sent than

letters via the post office. In a recent American Management Association

❹ surveying, _____ 36 percent of executives reported that ❺ you

_____ favor e-mail for most management ❻ communicate,

_____ compared with 26 percent who preferred the phone. (Surprisingly,

one of the less ❼ popular _____ alternatives was a face-to-face meeting,

favored by only 15 percent of the ❽ executives. One _____ executive

said, "❾ Its _____ only a matter of time before we do away with face-

to-face business deals ❿ complete _____.")

STUDENT ESSAY WRITING

In this section, you will go through the seven steps in writing a five-paragraph cause-effect essay. To review the details of each step, see Unit 1, pages 8–15.

| **Activity 19** | *Original Cause-Effect Essay* |

Using the seven steps that follow, write a five-paragraph cause-effect essay. Your teacher may assign a topic, you may think of one yourself, or you may choose from the suggestions in Step 1. You might need to do research.

Step 1: Choosing a Topic

Choose a topic that you understand well, including the causes and effects of the topic.

Suggestions:

Humanities:	Cause-effect essays are very popular in history courses. Choose a famous historical event (e.g., the American Revolution, the Civil Rights Movement) and explain what the causes of this event were.
Sciences:	Virtually all scientific experiments describe cause-effect relationships. Write an essay in which you describe a laboratory experiment that allows you to draw conclusions about the causes of a certain event.
Business:	All businesses desire the same effect: to sell more of their product. Develop a business model that explains how adopting certain marketing strategies will increase sales.
Personal narrative:	What were the reasons that you decided to attend the college you decided to attend? Write an essay that articulates the reasons (the causes) for your decision about which school to attend (the effect).

1. What topic did you choose? _____

2. Why did you choose this topic? _____

_____

_____

_____

_____

Step 2: Brainstorming

Use this space to jot down as many ideas about the topic as you can.

Brainstorming Box

Step 3: Outlining

Prepare a simple outline of your essay. Decide whether you will use the focus-on-causes method or the focus-on-effects method. Refer to the diagrams on pages 93–96.

Title: _____

(check one)   Type of cause-effect essay: __ focus-on-causes   __ focus-on-effects

I. Introduction _____

_____

Background information _____

_____

_____

Thesis statement: _____

_____

II. Point 1

_____

_____

III. Point 2

_____

_____

IV. Point 3

_____

_____

V. Conclusion _____

_____

Peer Editing of Outlines

Give your outline to a partner. This space is for your partner to write comments about your outline.

1. Is there anything in the outline that looks unclear to you?

_____

_____

_____

2. Can you think of an area in the outline that needs more development? Do you have any specific suggestions?

_____

_____

_____

3. If you have any other ideas or suggestions, write them here.

_____

_____

_____

Step 4: Writing the First Draft

Use the information from Steps 1–3 to write the first draft of your five-paragraph cause-effect essay.

Step 5: Peer Editing

Exchange essays with someone else. Read that person's essay and offer feedback on Peer Editing Sheet 4, pages 241–242.

Step 6: Revising Your Draft

Read the comments on Peer Editing Sheet 4 about your essay. Then reread your essay. Can you identify places where you plan to revise? List what you are going to do.

1. _____

_____

_____

2. _____

_____

_____

3. _____

_____

_____

Use all the information from the previous activities to write the final version of your paper. Writers will often need to write a third or even fourth draft to express their ideas clearly. Write as many drafts as necessary to produce a good essay.

Step 7: Proofing the Final Paper

Be sure to proofread your paper several times before you submit it.

TOPICS FOR WRITING

Here are ten topics for additional cause-effect essay writing.

TOPIC 1 ⟶ What are the effects of beauty or good looks?

TOPIC 2 ⟶ What are the causes of illiteracy?

TOPIC 3 ⟶ What are the effects of obesity?

TOPIC 4 ⟶ What are the effects of overcrowding, either in a university dormitory or in a city?

TOPIC 5 ⟶ Discuss how people's childhood experiences influence their lives.

TOPIC 6 ⟶ What effect can one person have on the government?

TOPIC 7 ⟶ What are the effects of sudden wealth (such as when a person wins the lottery)?

TOPIC 8 ⟶ What are the effects of poverty?

TOPIC 9 ⟶ What are the causes of happiness?

TOPIC 10 ⟶ What are the causes of a recent personal or political crisis?

 *Online Study Center*   For additional activities, go to the *Greater Essays* Online Study Center at http://esl.college.hmco.com/pic/greateressays1e

Persuasive Essays

Writing Goal:	To learn how to write a five-paragraph persuasive essay
Grammar Topic 5.1:	Preposition Combinations
Grammar Topic 5.2:	Verb Tense with *If* in Future Time
Grammar Topic 5.3:	*because* and *because of*
Grammar Topic 5.4:	Confusing Words: *to / too / two*
Grammar Topic 5.5:	Word Parts Practice

WHAT IS A PERSUASIVE ESSAY?

We frequently attempt to persuade our friends to agree with our viewpoints, whether the subject is which movie to watch or which vacation to take. In writing a persuasive essay, we use written words to achieve a similar goal. As the word "persuasive" suggests, writers of persuasive essays attempt to persuade, or convince, their readers to agree with them on a particular issue. By explaining their reasons for holding a particular belief, writers share their perceptions of an issue and hope to sway others to share this point of view.

Perhaps the most common type of persuasive essay is the newspaper editorial.* In these essays, writers pick an issue and explain its relevance to their readers. By educating their readers on a given topic, the writers hope to create a community of like-minded thinkers. For example, editorial writers often endorse particular candidates in local, state, and national elections; they want to persuade their readers to vote for the candidates who the writers think will do the best job.

At their best, persuasive essays clearly and logically explain a writer's reasons behind a given viewpoint. However, writers should not exaggerate their claims. It is better to be candid about the limitations of your viewpoint than to overstate the case.

*We strongly recommend reading an editorial in a newspaper of your choice to help you understand what persuasive writing is.

124

HOW IS A PERSUASIVE ESSAY ORGANIZED?

A persuasive essay is organized in the same general manner as the other essays we have studied throughout this book.

- It begins with an introductory paragraph in which the writer introduces the topic and thesis of the essay.

- The body paragraphs discuss the pros and cons of the thesis statement. For example, the first body paragraph might address the benefits of your position on an issue, and the second body paragraph might address the limitations of a counterposition. The third body paragraph might offer a compromise position between your position and the opposing point of view.

- The conclusion summarizes the state of the issue and restates your thesis.

WRITER'S NOTE: All Essays Are Persuasive Writing

All of the essay types in this book—process, comparison-contrast, cause-effect, persuasive, and narrative—can be seen as persuasive essays. When you write a narrative essay, you are convincing readers to see some aspect of your life in a certain way. Similarly, a process essay attempts to persuade the reader that this process is the most appropriate means of achieving a desired result. Comparison-contrast essays and cause-effect essays likewise persuade the reader that their thesis is a correct way of analyzing a given situation. When you write in any rhetorical mode, persuasion is always one of your goals. You want your reader to share your view of the world around you.

TOPICS FOR PERSUASIVE ESSAYS

What is a good topic for a persuasive essay? Obviously, it should be an issue that you feel strongly about and would like to share your opinions on. What is your opinion on the issue? Why do you feel this way? Can you think of some reasons that people might think differently than you do?

Here are some general topics that lend themselves well to a persuasive essay:

- stem cell research

- limiting oil exploration in national parks

- capital punishment

- mandatory military service

- raising the driving age

- merits of standardized testing

Activity 1   **Identifying Topics for Persuasive Essays**

Read these eight topics. Put a check (✓) next to the four that could be good topics for persuasive essays.

_____ 1. the first time I flew in a plane

_____ 2. whom to vote for in an upcoming mayoral election

_____ 3. how and why birds migrate south for the winter

_____ 4. steps in negotiating an international contract

_____ 5. the necessity of higher taxes on cigarettes

_____ 6. why schools should offer after-school programs for at-risk students

_____ 7. reasons that you deserve a raise at your job

_____ 8. how to play chess

Can you think of two additional topics that would be excellent for a persuasive essay?

9. _____

10. _____

Topic Details

After you have selected a topic, you will need to think about what you already know about the issue and what you need to find out. Asking yourself questions about both sides of the issue is a good way to generate details to include in your essay.

Activity 2   **Brainstorming Supporting Ideas**

Read the following thesis statements. What are three ideas to support it? Can you think of three ideas against it?

1. *Thesis statement:* Adults should be required to pass a test before they can be parents.

    Ideas for:

    a. _____

    b. _____

    c. _____

    Ideas against:

    a. _____

    b. _____

    c. _____

2. *Thesis statement:* The death penalty helps society to protect innocent people.

    Ideas for:

    a. _____

    b. _____

    c. _____

    Ideas against:

    a. _____

    b. _____

    c. _____

STUDYING A SAMPLE PERSUASIVE ESSAY

In this section, you will study three versions of a five-paragraph persuasive essay: a rough draft, the same rough draft with teacher comments, and the revised essay.

Activity 3	Warming Up to the Topic

Answer these questions individually. Then discuss them with a partner or in a small group.

1. How many e-mail accounts do you currently have? _____

2. How often do you check your e-mail? _____

3. About how many e-mails do you receive each day? How many of these e-mail messages are spam?

_____

4. Some people are so annoyed by spam that they want laws to punish spammers. Do you agree or

disagree with this idea? _____

Why or why not? Give two reasons.

a. _____

_____

_____

_____

b. _____

_____

_____

_____

Activity 4 **First Draft of the Essay**

As you read this rough draft, look for areas that need improvement.

Essay 5A   **Can Spam!**

When I first got an e-mail account ten years ago, I received

communications only from friends, family, and professional <u>acquaintances</u>.

Businesses do not contact to me with advertisements to sell me their services.

Now it seems that every time I check my e-mail, I have to delete a lot of

advertisements and other correspondence. I have no interest in reading this. If

we want e-mail to continue to be useful. We need laws that make criminal

spam. The <u>avalanche</u> of spam threaten to destroy this important means in

communication.

If the government will not do something soon to outlaw spam, the

problem will get much more bad. Computer programs allow spammers

sending hundreds of millions of e-mails virtually instantly. As more and more

advertisers turn to spam to sell their products, the e-mail that we want to

receive it could be greatly outnumbered for junk e-mail. Would you continue

to use e-mail if you had to delete 100 pieces spam for each e-mail that was

written to you by someone you know?

Companies rely with e-mail for their employees to communicate with

each other. Spamming corrupts their internal communications, and they are

unable to communicate effectively. Such a situation results with a lost of productivity for the company and requires sometimes the company to reformulate its communication network, to.

Despite of these problems for businesses, some people might discuss that criminalizing spam would infringe on spammers' right to free speech. However, how free is speech that drowns out another voices that we want to hear? The right to free speech does not allow companies to flood my mail box with its e-mail garbage. Yes, free speech is an <u>essential</u> component of the exchange with ideas necessary for <u>flourishing</u> democracy. Unsolicited e-mails, however, threaten to inhibit effective communication, not nurture it.

Because these reasons, our lawmakers need to legislate against spam. Spammers should be fined, and perhaps jailed, if they continue to disturb people with their <u>incessant</u> pleas of our attention and our money. E-mail was designed for be a helpful tool for allow people all over the world too communicate with each other quick and effective, but spam threatens to destroy this advance in the human communication.

can: throw away, eliminate

acquaintances: people whom one knows but who are not close friends

avalanche: a massive or overwhelming amount

essential: necessary

flourishing: thriving, healthy

incessant: constant

Activity 5 **Teacher Comments on First Draft**

Read the teacher comments on the first draft of "Can Spam!" Are these the same things that you noticed?

Essay 5B   **Can Spam!**   *The command in the title really grabs our attention*

When I first got an e-mail account ten years ago, I received

communications only from friends, family, and professional acquaintances.

Prep.

Businesses (do) not contact (to) me with advertisements to sell me their services.

use a more advanced

Now it seems that every time I check my e-mail, I have to delete (a lot of)   *word*

combine (embed)

advertisements and other correspondence. I have no interest in reading this. If

we want e-mail to continue to be useful. We need laws that (make criminal)

good vocab!   *Prep.*

spam. The avalanche of spam threaten to destroy this important means (in)

See how this phrase is so much better than the boring "a lot of"?

communication.

verb tense after "if"?

If the government will not do something soon to outlaw spam, the

problem will get much more bad. Computer programs allow spammers

(sending) hundreds of millions of e-mails virtually instantly. As more and more

advertisers turn to spam to sell their products, the e-mail that we want to

?   *Prep.*

receive (it) could be greatly outnumbered (for) junk e-mail. Would you continue

prep needed

to use e-mail if you had to delete 100 pieces spam for each e-mail that was

written to you by someone you know?

Mention computer viruses in   *Prep.*

this para.   Companies rely (with) e-mail for their employees to communicate with

Add transition

each other. Spamming corrupts their internal communications, and they are

Prep.   word form

unable to communicate effectively. Such a situation results (with) a (lost) of

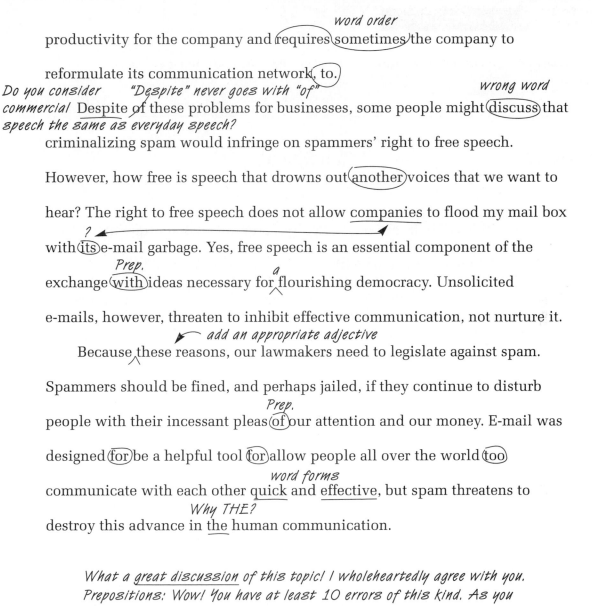

productivity for the company and requires sometimes the company to [*word order*]

reformulate its communication network, to.)

Do you consider   *"Despite" never goes with "of"*   *wrong word*
commercial Despite of these problems for businesses, some people might discuss that
speech the same as everyday speech?
criminalizing spam would infringe on spammers' right to free speech.

However, how free is speech that drowns out another voices that we want to

hear? The right to free speech does not allow companies to flood my mail box
?
with its e-mail garbage. Yes, free speech is an essential component of the
Prep.   *a*
exchange with ideas necessary for flourishing democracy. Unsolicited

e-mails, however, threaten to inhibit effective communication, not nurture it.
add an appropriate adjective
Because these reasons, our lawmakers need to legislate against spam.

Spammers should be fined, and perhaps jailed, if they continue to disturb
Prep.
people with their incessant pleas of our attention and our money. E-mail was

designed for be a helpful tool for allow people all over the world too
word forms
communicate with each other quick and effective, but spam threatens to
Why THE?
destroy this advance in the human communication.

What a great discussion of this topic! I wholeheartedly agree with you.
Prepositions: Wow! You have at least 10 errors of this kind. As you
revise, study the corrections. Prepositions are difficult, but the errors really
detract from the quality of your essay.
    Do you know the difference between because and because of? What about
the difference between despite and in spite of?
    I look forward to reading your next draft!

Activity 6   **Revised Essay**

Read the revised version of "Can Spam!" What has been changed? What still needs improvement?

Essay 5C   **Can Spam!**

When I first got an e-mail account ten years ago, I received communications only from friends, family, and professional acquaintances. Businesses did not contact me with advertisements to sell me their services. Now it seems that every time I check my e-mail, I have to delete an endless parade of advertisements and other correspondence that does not come from legitimate businesses and therefore does not interest me at all. If we want e-mail to continue to be useful, we need specific laws that criminalize spam. The annoying avalanche of spam threatens to destroy this important means of modern communication.

If the government does not do something soon to outlaw spam, the problem will certainly get much worse. Computer programs allow spammers to send hundreds of millions of e-mails virtually instantly. As more and more advertisers turn to spam to sell their products, the e-mail that we want to receive could be greatly outnumbered by junk e-mail. Would you continue to use e-mail if you had to delete 100 pieces of spam for each e-mail that was written to you by someone you know?

Although this problem with e-mail is troubling for private individuals, it is even worse for large businesses. Many spam e-mails contain computer viruses that can shut down the entire network of a business. Companies rely on e-mail for their employees to communicate with each other. Spamming corrupts their internal communications, and a company's employees are thus unable to communicate effectively. Such a situation results in a loss of productivity for the company and sometimes requires the company to reformulate its communication network, too. These computer problems raise the company's costs, which must then be passed on to the consumer.

Despite these problems for businesses, some people might argue that criminalizing spam would infringe on spammers' right to free speech. However, how free is speech that drowns out other voices that we want to hear? Commercial speech that is designed to encourage people to spend money is legally different from people's right to voice their personal opinions. The right to free speech does not allow companies to flood my mailbox with their e-mail garbage. Yes, free speech is an essential component of the exchange of ideas necessary for a flourishing democracy. Unsolicited e-mails, however, threaten to inhibit effective communication, not nurture it.

Because of these important reasons, our lawmakers need to legislate against spam. Spammers should be fined, and perhaps jailed, if they continue to disturb people with their incessant pleas for our attention and our money. E-mail was designed to be a helpful tool to allow people all over the world to communicate with each other quickly and effectively, but spam threatens to destroy this advance in human communication.

parade: a long procession of things
troubling: causing distress or worry

Analyzing Content and Organization

Activity 7   *Analyzing the Content*

Answer these questions about the revised version (5C) of "Can Spam!"

1. How many paragraphs does this essay have? _____

2. What is the topic? _____

3. Write the thesis statement here. _____

   _____

4. What reasons does the writer give for her viewpoint?

   _____

   _____

5. After reading this student's essay, do you agree with her viewpoint in the

   conclusion? Why or why not? _____

   _____

   _____

6. If you disagree with the thesis, what could the writer have done to make her
   point more convincing? If you agree with the thesis, think of some ways in
   which the writer could have been even more convincing.

   _____

   _____

   _____

7. Does the last sentence in the conclusion offer a suggestion, an opinion, or a prediction?

   _____

   _____

Activity 8   *Analyzing the Organization*

Read the outline of "Can Spam!" Then use information in the box to complete the outline.

- should be criminalized
- lose productivity
- the right to fill people's e-mail accounts with spam
- is growing
- background information

I. Introduction

    A. Give _____ about e-mail

    B. Demonstrate that e-mail advertisements ("spam") have become a problem

    C. Thesis: The avalanche of spam threatens to destroy this important means of communication.

II. Body Paragraph 1

    A. Show that the problem with spam _____

    B. Show that the problem with spam threatens the usefulness of e-mail as a means of communication

III. Body Paragraph 2

    A. Show that the problem is potentially even more troublesome for businesses than for individuals

    B. Discuss the ways in which businesses will _____

    _____ if employees spend time deleting spam

IV. Body Paragraph 3

    A. Address a likely counterargument that spam is a mode of free speech

    B. Demonstrate that a company's right to advertise does not give it

    _____

V. Conclusion

    A.   Suggest that spam _____

    B.   Offer a prediction about the effect of not criminalizing spam

TRANSITIONS AND CONNECTORS IN PERSUASIVE ESSAYS

Transitional phrases and connectors in persuasive essays help the reader to follow the logical development of the argument. When you move from one paragraph to the next to further develop a point, use a word or phrase from the following list of transitions that develop a point further. When you move from one paragraph to the next to address or refute a counterargument, use a word or phrase from the list of transitions that address a counterargument.

Transitions that develop a point further	Transitions that address a counterargument
additionally	although
also	but
besides	conversely
correspondingly	despite
furthermore	however
in a similar manner	in spite of
likewise	nevertheless
moreover	nonetheless
similarly	on the other hand
what is more	still
	though
	yet

Activity 9   Using Transitions and Connectors

Reread the revised version (5C) of "Can Spam!" on pages 134–135. Find and list four transitions or connectors and write the paragraph number after each.

1. _____ ( )   3. _____ ( )

2. _____ ( )   4. _____ ( )

VOCABULARY FOR BETTER WRITING

Vocabulary is important in writing. The following activities will help you to improve your knowledge and application of better vocabulary.

Activity 10	*Improving Your Vocabulary*

Circle the word or phrase to the right that is most closely related to the word on the left. The first one has been done for you

1. acquaintances	(people)	things
2. delete	add	subtract
3. parade	one person	many people
4. correspondence	spoken words	written words
5. criminalize	make illegal	make legal
6. virtually	almost	completely
7. outnumber	as many as	more than
8. troubling	it bothers you	you bother it
9. such	for example	for good
10. reformulate	do the form again	make a plan again
11. infringe	expand	limit
12. drown out	cover	reveal
13. essential	optional	required
14. flourishing	prospering	surprising
15. unsolicited	not requested	not understood

16. inhibit	provide	constrain
17. nurture	help to grow	persuade to act
18. fine	penalty payment	terrible treaty
19. incessant	irregular	unending
20. plea	strong request	strong punishment

Activity 11   *Using Collocations*

Fill in the blank with the word on the left that most naturally completes the phrase. The first one has been done for you.

1. work / natural
   _____ work _____ acquaintances

2. an old e-mail / a friend
   delete _____

3. satisfactory / perfect
   virtually _____

4. my family / my plan
   reformulate _____

5. noise / success
   drown out _____

6. candy / talk
   incessant _____

7. lengthy / one
   _____ correspondence

8. upon / with
   infringe _____

9. ingredient / mistake
   an essential _____

10. for / of
    a plea _____ assistance

11. needs / situation
    fulfill your _____

12. food / ideas
    _____ and shelter

GRAMMAR FOR BETTER WRITING

This section contains grammar that might be review for you or might be new. Grammatical errors in essays distract the reader and get in the way of clear communication. Your goal should be to create error-free essays. This section will help you to become a better editor of your own writing.

Grammar Topic 5.1	Preposition Combinations

Prepositions are one of the most difficult parts of speech to learn in almost any language. Many times, it is necessary to memorize preposition combinations of *verb + preposition*, *noun + preposition*, and *adjective + preposition*. You need to practice these important combinations.

verb + preposition:	*wait for, excel in, count on*
noun + preposition:	*the majority of, a need for, a solution to*
adjective + preposition:	*good at, excited about, proud of*

Activity 12 — *Working with Preposition Combinations*

Complete each sentence with a correct preposition. (Many of these word combinations can be found in "Can Spam!" [version 5C], pages 134–135.)

1. No businesses contacted me _____ advertisements to sell me their services.

2. an endless parade _____ advertisements

3. I have no interest _____ reading

4. hundreds _____ millions _____ e-mails

5. X is outnumbered _____ Y

6. 100 pieces _____ spam

7. e-mail that was written to you _____ someone you know

8. this problem is troubling _____ individuals

9. the potential _____ improvement

10. Companies rely _____ e-mail _____ their employees to

   communicate _____ each other.

11. a loss _____ productivity _____ the company

12. infringe _____ an advertiser's right _____ free speech

13. the exchange _____ ideas

14. it is necessary for the flourishing _____ a democracy

15. _____ these reasons

16. they continue to disturb us _____ their incessant pleas

   _____ our attention

Grammar Topic 5.2   **Verb Tense with *If* in Future Time**

In sentences with an *if*-clause, the *if*-clause is the condition. The other clause—the main clause—is the result.

condition   result

If I <u>delete</u> all my spam messages, <u>I</u> <u>will have</u> very few messages left.

Sentences with if-clauses can talk about the past, the present, or the future. When they talk about the future, the main clause expresses future tense with *will* or with *be going to*. However, the *if*-clause uses present tense to express what is clearly a future time.

present tense   future tense

If I <u>change</u> my e-mail address, <u>I will probably still get</u> spam. (future action)

Note: None of these uses of *if* involves contrary-to-fact situations.

Rule: In a sentence with an if-clause that expresses future time, use a future tense verb only in the main clause. Use a present tense verb in the if-clause.

A common use of *if* is in the present time. In this case, *if* is similar to *when* in meaning, and the verb in each clause is in the present tense.

> If I <u><u>receive</u></u> an e-mail from an unknown sender, I immediately <u><u>delete</u></u> it.

(present tense for a usual, repeated action)

For actions in the past, both clauses can use the past tense.

> If you <u><u>used</u></u> instant messaging, the other person <u><u>got</u></u> the message
>
> immediately.

Note: None of these uses of *if* involves contrary-to-fact situations.

| Activity 13 | **Working with Verb Tense with If** |

Each of the following sentences contains a verb tense error. Circle the error and write the correction on the line.

_____ 1. If something will not be done soon, the problem could get much worse.

_____ 2. If spamming will corrupt their internal communications, they will be

unable to communicate effectively.

_____ 3. Spammers should be fined, and perhaps jailed, if they will continue to

disturb people with their incessant pleas for our attention and our money.

_____ 4. If we will not do something about spam now, the problem will get much

worse before it gets better.

_____ 5. If people wanted to communicate with each other before 1980, they will

use the telephone or the post office.

Activity 14   Working with Real Language Use

Look in newspapers, in magazines, and on the Internet to locate three examples of sentences with if-clauses in future time. Write the examples below. Circle the verb in each clause and write its tense. Finally, identify the source of your sentences. Give the name of the source, its date, and the page number.

1. _____

   _____

   Verb tense of main clause: _____

   Verb tense of if-clause: _____

   Source information: _____

   _____

2. _____

   _____

   Verb tense of main clause: _____

   Verb tense of if-clause: _____

   Source information: _____

   _____

3. _____

   _____

   Verb tense of main clause: _____

   Verb tense of if-clause: _____

   Source information: _____

   _____

Grammar Topic 5.3   *because* and *because of*

Because is a conjunction. It connects a dependent clause to a main clause. (Any sentence that has a *because*-clause must have another clause.) The clause that begins with *because* can be at the beginning or the end of a sentence.

Rule 1: *Because* is followed by a subject + verb.

subject   verb

We need laws that criminalize spam **because** the <u>avalanche</u> of spam <u>threatens</u>

to destroy this important means of communication.

Rule 2: A sentence with a *because*-clause must have another clause.

Because the avalanche of spam threatens to destroy this important means

second clause

of communication, <u>we need laws that criminalize spam</u>.

Because of is a preposition. It must have a noun (or a pronoun) after it. The prepositional phrase with *because of* can be at the beginning or end of the sentence.

Rule 3: *Because of* is always followed by a noun or a pronoun.

noun

My favorite writer is William Shakespeare **because of** <u>the beautiful language</u>

noun

and <u>the strong characters</u> in his works.

Rule 4: The location of a clause with *because* or a phrase with *because of* can vary depending on how the sentence best fits in the paragraph or essay.

Because of the beautiful language and the strong characters in his works, my favorite writer is William Shakespeare.

OR

My favorite writer is William Shakespeare **because of** the beautiful language and the strong characters in his works.

Activity 15   **Working with Because *and* Because of**

Complete each sentence with because *or* because of.

1. I had to call my Internet provider _____ my e-mail account

   was filled with spam.

2. At times, users may receive a message that says, "Your Internet connection was

   interrupted _____ a program error or user inactivity."

3. _____ Internet glitches, the Microsoft Corporation had no

   choice but to withdraw a security improvement.

4. As the year 2000 approached, the U.S. Pentagon beefed up computer security

   tremendously _____ a Pentagon belief that attacks on it

   would increase.

5. Spam is a tremendous financial nuisance to carriers and recipients of the

   messages _____ most of the costs are incurred by the carriers

   and recipients instead of the senders.

6. One of the largest Internet providers in North America recently began to

   block e-mail from a company called Nordlain _____ the

   provider had received numerous complaints from its subscribers about spam

   being sent to them from Nordlain addresses.

7. A recent study has found that 30% of survey respondents indicated that they

   use e-mail less _____ the alarming wave of spam that is

   flooding into Internet users' boxes.

8. _____ no spam filter is perfect, it is likely that spam will

   continue to be a problem for all Internet users.

Grammar Topic 5.4   Confusing Words: *to / too / two*

The words *to*, *too*, and *two* sound alike, but they are used very differently. Do not confuse them in your writing.

to =	preposition	The plan will give more money **to** schools.
	infinitive	If voters want better schools, they have **to pay** more taxes.
too =	adverb (means *also*)	Our plan is weak, and their plan is weak, **too.**
	adverb (means *very*)	If taxes are **too** high, voters may be angry.
two =	a number	There were **two** possible ways to solve the problem.

Activity 16   *Working with Confusing Words: to / too / two*

Complete each sentence with to, too, *or* two.

1. What can we do _____ solve the problem of spam?

2. Please submit _____ copies of your application. One should go _____ the registrar, and the other should go _____ your advisor.

3. If _____ people apply for the same job, a committee of five meets _____ decide _____ whom they should give the position.

4. If you would like _____ support this plan because you believe that it is _____ risky _____ continue with our current situation, then please sign this petition. If you have friends or acquaintances who might be interested in this, please ask them to sign, _____.

Grammar Topic 5.5   **Word Parts Practice**

You can increase your vocabulary in two basic ways. One is to learn words that you have never seen before. The second is to learn word parts, which will help you to understand how other words are constructed. Recognizing word parts and using them correctly will increase your vocabulary and thus improve your writing.

Activity 17   *Editing Word Parts*

Read the following paragraph. Five of the eight underlined words contain an error with word parts. Correct the error or write C (correct). If you need more information about words parts, review Appendix 3, pages 218–220. The first one has been done for you

Personal interviews are generally considered to be one of the most ❶ <u>validity</u>

_____ valid _____ methods of survey research. In a ❷ <u>personal</u>

_____ interview, the ❸ <u>interview</u> _____ can

probe, ask for ❹ <u>clarification</u> _____, clear up any misunderstandings

❺ <u>immediate</u> _____, ensure that all questions are answered

completely, and pursue ❻ <u>unexpect</u> _____ avenues. Thus, data

❼ <u>result</u> _____ from an interview are often of a higher ❽ <u>quality</u>

_____ than data resulting from a questionnaire.

Activity 18   *Review of Grammar Topics 5.1–5.5*

Seven of the following ten sentences contain an error involving one of the grammar topics featured in this unit. Write a C before the three correct sentences. Write X before the incorrect sentences, circle the error, and write a correction above it.

_____ 1. The number of spam e-mails is certainly a problem, but the obscene

content of many of these messages is a problem, to.

_____ 2. If your computer seems to have a problem with a virus, you should get in

contact with your local computer repair shop as soon as possible.

_____ 3. The spectators at the gymnastics competition expressed their disapproval

because the extremely low score that the judges awarded.

_____ 4. If there will be sufficient demand for a new type of spam blocker, one of

the major computer companies will market it.

_____ 5. It is a teacher's job to teach well, but ultimately students are responsible to

how much they are able to learn in a course.

_____ 6. Because the manufacturer's decision to cut product prices in half,

consumers now have the opportunity to purchase a great new car at a

very reasonable price.

_____ 7. Because of a major increase in the number of people using the Internet,

e-mail has become the main means of communication for many people.

_____ 8. Disappointed with his team's performance in the match, the coach

blamed the loss on the poor performance of three key players.

_____ 9. Because of people were becoming annoyed with the amount of spam in

their e-mail accounts, they asked their government officials to pass some

kind of law to solve their dilemma.

_____ 10. The dentist told her patient, "Take one of these tablets for the next week.

Come back for a follow-up visit next Wednesday. If you will have any

problems between now and then, call us immediately."

| **Activity 19** | *Editing a Paragraph: Review of Grammar Topics 5.1–5.5* |

Seven of the ten underlined words in the following paragraph contain an error involving one of the grammar topics featured in this unit. Correct the errors on the lines provided. If the word or phrase is correct, write C.

Advertising programs in foreign markets need ❶ <u>to</u> _____ take a

number of key ❷ <u>considers</u> _____ into account. First, a broad vision of

sales in international markets is a requirement. This means, among other things, that overseas

markets must be viewed with promise if the marketing challenges are to be properly

faced. Second, international advertising rarely succeeds if it ❸ <u>will be</u>

_____ merely a duplicate ❹ <u>of</u> _____ advertising

used in the United States. ❺ <u>Traditional</u> _____, religions, and economic conditions may dictate the **❻** natural _____ of the sales appeal.

Illustrations should fit local conditions with respect **❼** about _____

such matters as color preferences and taboos. Advertising in India, for example, should never

show the cow **❽** because of _____ it is a sacred animal. Finally,

difficulties in translation must be considered, **❾** too _____.

Communication can be **❿** serious _____ impaired and even prevented if

a single word is mistranslated.

STUDENT ESSAY WRITING

In this section, you will go through the seven steps in writing a five-paragraph persuasive essay. To review the details of each step, see Unit 1, pages 8–15.

| Activity 20 | _Original Persuasive Essay_ |

Using the seven steps that follow, write a five-paragraph persuasive essay. Your teacher may assign a topic, you may think of one yourself, or you may choose from the suggestions in Step 1. You might need to do research.

Step 1: Choosing a Topic

Choose a topic for persuasion that you understand well, including both sides of the issue.

Suggestions:

Humanities:	Present an argument about the quality of a recent movie. Should your readers see the movie or not?
Sciences:	Is it ethical to clone animals? Write a persuasive essay that addresses this topic.
Business:	Describe the best strategies that managers should use to motivate their employees.
Personal:	Who is your personal hero? Explain why this person inspires you.

1. What topic did you choose? _____

2. Why did you choose this topic? _____

_____

_____

Step 2: Brainstorming

Use this space to jot down as many ideas about the topic as you can.

Brainstorming Box

```


```

Step 3: Outlining

Prepare a simple outline of your essay. (This outline is for five paragraphs, but you may have more or fewer if your teacher approves.)

Title: _____

I. Introduction _____

_____

Background information _____

_____

Thesis statement: _____

_____

II. Point 1

_____

_____

III. Point 2

_____

_____

IV. Point 3

_____

_____

V. Conclusion _____

_____

Peer Editing of Outlines

Give your outline to a partner. This space is for your partner to write comments about your outline.

1. Is there anything in the outline that looks unclear to you?

_____

_____

_____

2. Can you think of an area in the outline that needs more development? Do you have any specific suggestions?

_____

_____

_____

3. If you have any other ideas or suggestions, write them here.

_____

_____

_____

Step 4: Writing the First Draft

Use the information from Steps 1–3 to write the first draft of your five-paragraph persuasive essay.

Step 5: Peer Editing

Exchange essays with someone else. Read that person's essay and offer feedback on Peer Editing Sheet 5, pages 243–244.

Step 6: Revising Your Draft

Read the comments on Peer Editing Sheet 5 about your essay. Then reread your essay. Can you identify places where you plan to revise? List what you are going to do.

1. _____

_____

_____

_____

2. _____

_____

_____

3. _____

_____

_____

Use all the information from the previous activities to write the final version of your paper. Writers will often need to write a third or even a fourth draft to express their ideas clearly. Write as many drafts as necessary to produce a good essay.

Step 7: Proofing the Final Paper

Be sure to proofread your paper several times before you submit it.

TOPICS FOR WRITING

Here are ten topics for additional persuasive essay writing.

TOPIC 1 ➡ Why the U.S. Constitution should or should not be amended to allow U.S. citizens born outside of the United States to run for president

TOPIC 2 ➡ Why computers in public libraries should or should not have Internet filters installed

TOPIC 3 ➡ Why your class should take a field trip to a particular place

TOPIC 4 ➡ Why television shows should or should not be allowed to use obscene language

TOPIC 5 ➡ Why the drinking age should or should not be lowered to 18

TOPIC 6 ➡ Why the military draft should or should not be reinstated

TOPIC 7 ➡ Why public schools should or should not offer bilingual programs

TOPIC 8 ➡ Why junk food manufacturers should or should not be allowed to advertise their products to children

TOPIC 9 ➡ Why a friend of yours should or should not enroll in your college

TOPIC 10 ➡ Why health care should or should not be provided by the government

Online Study Center   For additional activities, go to the *Greater Essays* Online Study Center at http://esl.college.hmco.com/pic/greateressays1e

Narrative Essays

WHAT IS A NARRATIVE ESSAY?

A narrative essay is a nonfictional account of an experience. Narrative essays could describe a trip that you took or a particular memory from your childhood. A narrative essay might tell a story about your family or explain how a certain event influenced your development into the person that you are now. You have as many narrative essays to write as you have lifetime experiences. Through narrative essays, writers explain their personal reasons for the ways in which they perceive the world.

HOW IS A NARRATIVE ESSAY ORGANIZED?

As with any essay, a narrative essay has a thesis statement so that its relevance and meaning is apparent to the reader. You could write a narrative essay about going to the store to buy butter, but unless something truly unexpected or remarkable happened during the errand, this life experience is not the most interesting one to describe. Narrative essays are more interesting and enjoyable when the writers share the reason that the experience is important to their growth and maturity. This reason should be the thesis of your essay.

Narrative essays contain an introduction, supporting body paragraphs, and a conclusion. The body of a narrative essay tells the plot of your story and gives supporting details and evidence to bolster the thesis of the essay. Since narrative essays tell a story, you also need to consider these additional elements:

Setting: the location of the narrative. Where does the story take place?

Main characters: the people described in the narrative essay. Who are the essential actors in the story?

Plot: the action and events of the narrative essay. What happened to the main characters?

Climax: the most interesting or exciting point of the plot. What is the narrative essay's single most dramatic, tense, or engaging moment?

Ending: the resolution of the story, also called the dénouement. How are the issues in the plot resolved?

TOPICS FOR NARRATIVE ESSAYS

What is a good topic for a narrative essay? What are the stories about your life that you find yourself telling over and over? The answers to these two questions are the same. A narrative is a story, so the topic of a narrative essay should tell about an interesting or significant event in your life.

Here are some general topics that lend themselves well to a narrative essay:

- a family holiday

- a special vacation or trip

- the first time you did something, such as skiing or wallpapering a room

- an unexpected event

- something you learned a lesson from

Activity 1   **Identifying Appropriate Topics for Narrative Essays**

Read these eight topics. Put a check (✓) next to the four that could be good topics for narrative essays.

_____ 1. the steps in making my favorite dish

_____ 2. my brother's wedding day

_____ 3. my experience as a babysitter

_____ 4. illustrations in children's storybooks

_____ 5. an argument against cloning

_____ 6. a soldier's first week in battle

_____ 7. the history of a foreign country

_____ 8. disasters during a family vacation

Can you think of two additional topics that would be excellent for a narrative essay?

9. _____

10. _____

Topic Details

   After you have selected the topic of your narrative essay, your task is to identify the **setting, main characters, plot, climax,** and **ending.** This process will also help you to identify supporting details for your essay. What are the details of the event that make it interesting and unique? What would readers like to learn about the topic?

Activity 2   **Brainstorming for a Narrative Essay**

Do you have a favorite story from your childhood? Can you think of an important and memorable event in your life? Use one or both of the boxes below to write some ideas about a story from your life. Be sure to include the reason that you like this story. Can this reason become the thesis statement of your essay?

an important and memorable event in your life	
a list of steps that happened	
why you like this story and why it is important to you	

You can brainstorm the same information in terms of the parts of a story.

Setting	
Main Characters	
Plot	
Climax	
Ending	

STUDYING A SAMPLE NARRATIVE ESSAY

In this section, you will study three versions of a five-paragraph narrative essay: a rough draft, the same rough draft with teacher comments, and the revised essay.

Activity 3   *Warming Up to the Topic*

Answer these questions individually. Then discuss them with a partner or in a small group.

1. Why do people learn a second language? _____
_____

2. What are some reasons that people do not succeed at learning a second language?

_____

_____

_____

3. How do you think learning a second language is different now from the way it was one hundred

years ago? _____

_____

_____

Activity 4   **First Draft of the Essay**

As you read this rough draft, look for areas that need improvement.

Essay 6A   **Why I Learned English**

My family's roots are mixed and <u>intertwined</u> with several different <u>ethnic</u> and culture background. My mother's parents are American, but her ancestors are origin from England and German. My father's mother is Peruvian, but his father is Egyptian. I grew up in Peru with my parents in a quiet neighborhood of Lima. My <u>paternal</u> grandparents lived down the street from us, but my <u>maternal</u> grandparents lived in America. I didn't learn English for school; I learned English so that I spoke to my grandparents.

When my maternal grandparents would fly from North America to South America to visit us, my mother had to translate among the different family members. We spoke Spanish in our house, but my American grandparents spoke only English. Since he did not speak a word of Spanish. My mother was constantly <u>interpreting</u> questions and answers. I hated this translation step so much that I was determined that one day I will be able to speak to my grandparents by myself.

Eventually, this situation reached its <u>boiling point</u>. One day my mother asked to my grandmother to pick me up from school. My school was only a few blocks from our house. But my grandmother got horrible lost in the way. She ended up in the wrong neighborhood. She had to get help from the police. Now we all realized that being <u>monolingual</u> was a huge <u>handicap</u>. In addition, it was a potential dangerous handicap!

The next time my grandparents came to visit, I taped vocabulary cards on all of the objects in our house. On the *silla*, I hung a card with "chair" written on it. On the *mesa*, I attached a card that said "table." I continued putting these English words in the house. Meanwhile, my grandparents saw how hardly I was working for learn English, and they had decided that they wanted to learn Spanish. Later, we wrote the Spanish words on all of the cards as well so that we could practice together. Most of the cards we're yellow, and I used a green pen to write the words. My mom would help us with grammar whenever we had questions. It was so much fun to turn our monolingual Spanish house into a truly bilingual home.

During I was studying English, I realized that learn a language does more than teach you the new words; it ables you to learn about the new people. Instead of need my mother to say me stories about my grandparents, we can now talk direct each other. By learn new things, you can to experience new relationships.

---

intertwined: joined by twisting together

ethnic: relating to a group of people who share the same racial, national, religious, linguistic, or cultural background

paternal: related through one's father

maternal: related through one's mother

interpreting: explaining the meaning

boiling point: critical moment, climax

monolingual: using only one language

handicap: something that gets in the way

Activity 5   **Teacher Comments on First Draft**

Read the teacher comments on the first draft of "Why I Learned English." Are these the same things that you noticed?

Essay 6B   **Why I Learned English**

What about a more generic intro so you can move from PEOPLE to YOUR FAMILY to YOU?

redundant

My family's roots are (mixed and intertwined) with several different ethnic

word forms   and (culture) (background). My mother's parents are American, but her ancestors

adverb   are <u>origin</u> from England and German. My father's mother is Peruvian, but his

father is Egyptian. I grew up in Peru with my parents in a quiet neighborhood

of Lima. My paternal grandparents lived down the street from us, but my

maternal grandparents lived in America. I didn't learn English for school; I

add modal "could"

learned English so that I (spoke) to my grandparents.

This para. needs a topic sentence.   When my maternal grandparents would fly from North America to South

America to visit us, my mother had to translate among the different family

members. We spoke Spanish in our house, but my American grandparents

FRAG

spoke only English. <u>Since (he) did not speak a word of Spanish.</u> My mother

was constantly interpreting questions and answers. I hated this translation

tense?

step so much that I was determined that one day I (will) be able to speak to my

grandparents by myself.

Eventually, this situation reached its boiling point. One day my mother

asked (to) my grandmother to pick me up from school. My school was only a

combine   *word form   prep*

few blocks from our house. But my grandmother got (horrible) lost (in) the way.

combine-choppy

She ended up in the wrong neighborhood. She had to get help from the

police. Now we all realized that being monolingual was a huge <u>handicap</u>. In

addition, it was a (potential) dangerous <u>handicap</u>!   *Put this info in previous sentence*

Connect this idea more directly to your thesis about
learning languages in your previous paragraph.

∧The next time my grandparents came to visit, I taped vocabulary cards on

Transition sentence? This is a huge leap

all of the objects in our house. On the *silla*, I hung a card with "chair" written

on it. On the *mesa*, I attached a card that said "table." I continued putting

all over?

these English words <u>in</u> the house. Meanwhile, my grandparents saw how

why past perfect?

hard(ly) I was working (for) learn English, and they <u>had decided</u> that they

wanted to learn Spanish. Later, we wrote the Spanish words on all of the

Is this important?

cards as well so that we could practice together. <u>Most of the cards (we're)</u> *relevant?*

Can you

<u>yellow, and I used a green pen to write the words.</u> My mom would help us *develop /*
use it

with grammar whenever we had questions. It was so much fun to turn our *better in*
the essay?

monolingual Spanish house into a truly bilingual home.

word choice?   *word form*

<u>During</u> I was studying English, I realized that l(earn) a language does more

not a verb

than teach you the new words; it <u>ables</u> you to learn about t̶h̶e new people.

word form   *word choice*

Instead of ne(ed) my mother to <u>say</u> me stories about my grandparents, we can

now talk dire(ct) each other. By lea(rn) new things, you can to experience new

relationships.

This is an interesting story. It's easy for your reader to follow.
My main suggestion to improve your writing is to combine some of
your sentences.
You have 2 fragments—serious errors. If you need help with
fragments, see grammar point 4.2 in this textbook.

Activity 6   **Revised Essay**

Read the revised version of "Why I Learned English." What has been changed? What still needs improvement?

Essay 6C   Why I Learned English

Many families reflect diverse cultural backgrounds that come together. My family's roots are intertwined with several different ethnic and cultural backgrounds. My mother's parents are American, but her ancestors are originally from England and Germany. My father's mother is Peruvian, but his father is Egyptian. I grew up in Peru with my parents in a quiet neighborhood of Lima. My paternal grandparents lived down the street from us, but my maternal grandparents lived in the United States. Unlike most non-native speakers, I did not learn English for school; I learned English so that I could speak to my grandparents.

Coming from a multilingual family sparked many difficulties in communication. For example, when my maternal grandparents would fly from North America to South America to visit us, my mother had to translate among the different family members. We spoke Spanish in our house, but my American grandparents spoke only English. Since they did not speak a word of Spanish, my mother was constantly interpreting questions and answers. Rather than enjoying their visit, my mother had to work as a translator. With my mom's help, I could understand my grandparents, but I wanted to be able to speak to them by myself.

Eventually, this situation reached its boiling point. One day my mother asked my grandmother to pick me up from school. My school was only a few blocks from our house, but my grandmother got horribly lost on the way. She ended up in the wrong neighborhood and had to get help from the police. It was quite embarrassing for a grown woman to find herself lost in a small neighborhood. Now we all realized that being monolingual was a huge handicap. In addition, it was a potentially dangerous liability!

Because of this incident, I decided to take action. The next time my grandparents came to visit, I taped vocabulary cards on all of the objects in our house. On the *silla*, I hung a card with "chair" written on it. On the *mesa*, I attached a card that said "table." I continued putting these English words all over the house. Meanwhile, my grandparents saw how hard I was working to learn English, and they decided that they wanted to learn Spanish. Later, we wrote the Spanish words on all of the cards as well so that we could practice together. My mom would help us with grammar whenever we had questions. It was so much fun to turn our monolingual Spanish house into a truly bilingual home.

While I was studying English, I realized that learning a language does more than teach you new words; it enables you to learn about new people. Instead of needing my mother to tell me stories about my grandparents, we can now talk directly to each other. Now my grandparents and I talk on the phone every week without a translator, and our relationship is much closer than it ever was before. By learning a common language to communicate, you can experience new relationships.

liability: a disadvantage or handicap

Analyzing Content and Organization

Activity 7   *Analyzing the Content*

Answer these questions about the revised version (6C) of "Why I Learned English."

1. Why does the narrator want to learn English? _____

_____

_____

2. How well does the first sentence of the essay grab your attention? Does it make you want to

   read the rest? _____

_____

_____

3. What is the setting of this narrative essay? Who are the main characters?

_____

_____

_____

4. What is the plot of this narrative essay? What is its climax?

_____

_____

_____

5. Does the essay have a thesis? What do you think the writer wants you to learn from reading

   her essay? _____

_____

_____

Activity 8 | *Analyzing the Organization*

Read the outline of "Why I Learned English." Then use the information in the box to complete this outline for the essay.

> - Body paragraph 3
> - the importance of learning a foreign language
> - I could not communicate with my grandparents
> - characters
> - my grandmother got lost

I. Introduction

    A. Provide background information about my family heritage

    B. Introduce the setting and _____

    C. Thesis: My family heritage made learning English essential

II. Body paragraph 1. Establish the conflict of the plot: _____

_____

III. Body paragraph 2. Describe the climax: when _____

_____

IV. _____ . Tell the resolution and the solutions that we used to solve

our problem

V. Conclusion

    A. Summarize _____

    B. Explain how a person becomes open to new experiences with a new language

TRANSITIONS AND CONNECTORS IN NARRATIVE ESSAYS

The most commonly used transitions and connectors in narrative essays are time words and phrases. Because a narrative essay tells a story, the transitions need to show sequence.

after	following	one day
after that	from … to …	soon
at first	last	then
before	later	until
during	meanwhile	when
eventually	next, the next time	whenever
finally	now	while

Activity 9   *Using Transitions and Connectors*

Reread the revised version (6C) of "Why I Learned English" on pages 166–167. Find and list eight transitions or connectors and write the paragraph number after each. One has been done for you.

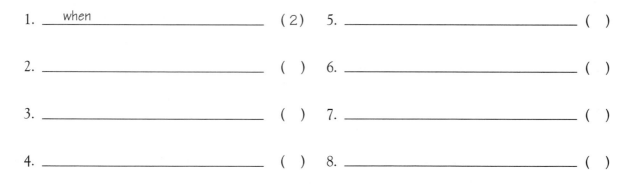

1. __when_____ (2)   5. _____ ( )

2. _____ ( )   6. _____ ( )

3. _____ ( )   7. _____ ( )

4. _____ ( )   8. _____ ( )

VOCABULARY FOR BETTER WRITING

Vocabulary is important in writing. The following activities will help you to improve your knowledge and application of better vocabulary.

Activity 10   *Improving Your Vocabulary*

Circle the word or phrase to the right that is most closely related to the word on the left. The first one has been done for you.

1. mixed	(together)	separate
2. intertwined	wrapped together	remembered many details
3. ethnic	groups of people	groups of languages
4. cultural	plants	people
5. background	heritage	future
6. paternal	related to one's father	related to one's mother
7. maternal	related to one's father	related to one's mother
8. translate	maintain	change
9. constantly	sometimes	always
10. interpret	translate	liability
11. situation	enjoyment	predicament
12. boiling point	climax	anger
13. blocks	neighborhoods	neighbors
14. monolingual	one language	many languages
15. handicap	asset	disability
16. potentially	gradually	possibly
17. grammar	language	cars
18. bilingual	two languages	two situations
19. enables	makes difficult	makes possible
20. relationships	families	corporations

Activity 11   *Using Collocations*

Fill in the blank with the word on the left that most naturally completes the phrase. The first one has been done for you.

1. across / through   flew _____ across _____ the ocean

2. down / over   lived _____ the street

3. up / on   pick me _____

4. reach / take   _____ a boiling point

5. into / above   to turn _____

6. to / you   it enables _____

7. of / for   instead _____

8. other / another   to each _____

9. from / over   originally _____ England

10. in / sometimes   grew up _____

11. cultural / quiet   a _____ neighborhood

12. to / from   speak _____ her

13. of / to   a word _____ Spanish

14. able / can   to be _____ to speak

15. from / without   a few blocks _____ our house

16. up / over   ended _____ in the wrong neighborhood

17. from / of   get help _____ the police

18. dangerous / translated   potentially _____

19. with / of   help us _____

20. about / over   to learn _____

GRAMMAR FOR BETTER WRITING

This section contains grammar that might be review for you or might be new. Grammatical errors in essays distract the reader and get in the way of clear communication. Your goal should be to create error-free essays. This section will help you to become a better editor of your own writing.

Grammar Topic 6.1	Unclear Pronoun and the Word It Refers to

When you use a pronoun, make sure that the reader knows which previous noun the pronoun refers to. If the pronoun's reference is ambiguous, use a noun.

Unclear: The banker told the customer that **he** could not accept coins, only paper money.

(Who is *he*? The banker? The customer?)

Clear: The banker told **the customer**, "I will not accept coins, only paper."

Unclear: **They** say that aspirin can help to prevent heart attacks.

(Who is *they*?)

Clear: **Doctors** say that aspirin can help to prevent heart attacks.

Unclear: Congress passed the new law on July 17, **which** was surprising.

(What was surprising? The date? The law? The fact that Congress passed the law?)

Clear: It was surprising that **Congress passed the new law on July 17.**

Or: **The new law that Congress passed on July 17** was surprising.

Unclear: **They** may approve a contract for a new book when the authors submit a detailed summary of their proposed book.

(Who is *they*? The authors? The publishers?)

Clear: **Publishers** may approve a contract for a new book when the authors submit a detailed summary of their proposed book.

Unclear: "May I help you? We have hot dogs, hamburgers, and cheeseburgers." "Yes, give me **one**."

(What is *one*? A hot dog? A hamburger? A cheeseburger?)

Clear: "May I help you? We have hot dogs, hamburgers, and cheeseburgers." "Yes, give me a **cheeseburger**."

The correct possessive adjective when referring to *each*, *someone*, *somebody*, *anyone*, *anybody*, *everyone*, and *everybody* is *his* (or *her*). In conversational English, you will hear people use *their*, but this is not acceptable in formal academic writing.

Informal: Someone left **their** umbrella here.

Formal: Someone left **his** umbrella here.

Or: Someone left **his or her** umbrella here.

Best: Someone left an umbrella here.

(Using a possessive adjective with general nouns such as *someone* or *everybody* is awkward. *Their* is incorrect in formal writing. *His* is sexist. *His or her* is awkward and wordy. The best solution is to avoid this construction when possible.)

Activity 12   **Working with Unclear Pronoun Reference**

Rewrite these sentences to create clear pronoun references.

1. When Michael drove his truck through the garage door, he damaged it.

   _____

2. When the Prince finds Cinderella, it means that they can live happily ever after.

   _____

3. If your dog will not eat its food, then give it to the cat.

_____

4. In today's job market, a college graduate can find a good job more easily than a person who does not have one.

_____

5. Both Susan Jennings and Kathy Miller teach at a college in Vermont. She is a professor of English.

_____

6. They think that the criminal might have murdered as many as seven people.

_____

7. Once everyone has their pencils sharpened, we may begin.

_____

8. Mr. Johnston made his special barbecued chicken, which we appreciated.

_____

9. Last month the pilot flew to Rio and the following week to Paris. It is his favorite flight.

_____

10. The professor verified whether or not everyone had done their homework.

_____

Grammar Topic 6.2   Expressing Past Time: Past, Past Progressive, Past Perfect

There are several ways of expressing past time in English.

Past Tense

The most commonly used verb tense is the simple past. It often ends in *-ed* (*showed*) but can be irregular (*went*).

> In 1975, Home Depot **opened** many stores in this area of the country.

> In the twentieth century, automobiles **began** to shape American life.

Past Progressive Tense

This tense consists of *was* or *were* plus the verb + *-ing* form (*was eating, were playing*). The past progressive is used when a second action (expressed in simple past) interrupts the flow of the action.

> The children **were playing** outside when the lightning storm **arrived**.

Past Perfect Tense

This tense consists of *had* plus the past participle form of the verb (*had eaten, had opened*). The past perfect tense is generally used in two cases.

1. When one past action occurred before another past action

> Zachary received a B+ on his test today because he **had studied** for three
>
> days in a row.

> Or: Zachary received a B+ on his test today because he studied for three
>
> days in a row.

Note: The past perfect is often optional here because it is clear to the reader which of the two actions happened first.

2. In *if*-clauses to describe a past unreal condition

> If Zachary **had studied** during the whole semester, he probably would have
>
> received an A.

Note: The past perfect is always mandatory here.

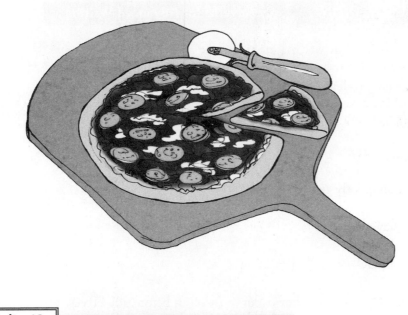

Activity 13   *Working with Past Tense Forms*

Read this paragraph about a famous pizza company. Underline the correct verb in each set of parentheses.

Before launching a new product, Domino's Pizza ❶ (gathers, gathered, had gathered)

data by asking selected groups of people about the concept and the taste. For example, before

introducing the Roma Herb-flavored crust pizza, the company ❷ (elicits, elicited, was eliciting)

comments from groups of consumers, analyzed the results, and then ❸ (invites, invited, was

inviting, had invited) other groups to taste and discuss various samples. Finally, Domino's

❹ (tests, tested, was testing, had tested) actual customer response by offering the product in

a limited number of stores before the company ❺ (makes, made, was making, had made) it

available throughout the United States.

Grammar Topic 6.3   ***-ly* Adverbs for Advanced Writing**

One of the best ways to make your writing more precise and at the same time sound more formal and advanced is through the use of adverbs of manner and degree. The form of these adverbs is easy to learn: they end in *-ly*.

Adverbs of manner tell *how*.

adverb   adverb   verb

The thief **quickly** and **quietly** <u>entered</u> the building.

verb adverb

The project <u>ended</u> **badly**.

Adverbs of degree tell to what extent. They occur most often before adjectives, especially past participles used as adjectives. Instead of using the common word *very* in your essays, make your writing more original by using other adverbs of degree:

adequately	greatly	practically
completely	immensely	profoundly
entirely	internationally	thoroughly
especially	partially	tremendously
extremely	particularly	virtually

adverb   adjective (past participle)

The audience was **thoroughly** <u>disgusted</u> by the speaker's remarks.

adverb   adjective (past participle)

Tracy Jenks is an **internationally** <u>recognized</u> expert in antiterrorism.

Activity 14	*Working with Adverbs*

Underline the correct word in each set of parentheses.

In a company, how should bad news be reported to employees? The **❶** (bad, badly) news is communicated up front in **❷** (direct, directly) written messages. Even in an **❸** (indirect, indirectly) written message, if you have done a **❹** (convincing, convincingly) job of explaining the reasons, the bad news itself will **❺** (natural, naturally) come as no surprise; the decision will appear **❻** (logical, logically) and reasonable—indeed the only logical and **❼** (reasonable, reasonably) decision that could have been made under the circumstances. To retain the reader's goodwill, state the bad news in **❽** (positive, positively) or **❾** (neutral, neutrally) language, stressing what you are able to do rather than what you are not able to do. In addition, put the bad news in the middle of a paragraph and include additional discussion of reasons in the same sentence or **❿** (immediate, immediately) afterward.

WRITER'S NOTE: *Remember to Include -ly Adverbs*

When you want to advance your writing, use *-ly* adverbs. Remember that *-ly* adverbs include both adverbs of manner (e.g., *slowly, carefully*) and adverbs of degree (*extremely, completely*).

Grammar Topic 6.4	**Confusing Words: *we're / were / where***

The words *we're*, *were*, and *where* sound similar, but they are used very differently. Do not confuse them in your writing.

we're = we are	**We're** planning to return these books to the library today.
were = past of *be*	The boxes **were** empty when we found them.
where = a place	No one knows **where** the court trial will take place.

Activity 15   *Working with Confusing Words: we're / were / where*

Complete each of the following sentences with we're, were, or where.

1. _____ ready to take the children to the cinema, but we do

   not know _____ it is located.

2. The police want to know _____ the men

   _____ last night.

3. I do not know why you could not find us this morning. Sheila and I

   _____ _____ we told you that we would be

   waiting for you.

4. We have to hurry. If _____ late again, we will be fired.

5. Most of the discussions _____ about the place

   _____ next year's meeting will take place.

Grammar Topic 6.5   **Word Parts Practice**

You can increase your vocabulary in two basic ways. One is to learn words that you have never seen before. The second is to learn word parts, which will help you to understand how other words are constructed. Recognizing word parts and using them correctly will increase your vocabulary and thus improve your writing.

Activity 16
Editing Word Parts

Read the paragraph. Five of the eight underlined words contain an error with word parts. Correct the error or write C (correct). If you need more information about word parts, review Appendix 3, pages 218–220. The first one has been done for you.

A solid has a **❶** <u>fixed</u> _____*C*_____ shape that bears no **❷** <u>related</u>

_____ to the shape of the container holding it. (A collection of

small pieces may adopt the shape of the **❸** <u>contain</u> _____, however.)

When solids are placed under pressure, they do not change their volume to a

❹ <u>significantly</u> _____ extent; for example, a piece of wood does not

decrease **❺** <u>noticeable</u> _____ in volume when it is squeezed.

In other words, solids have low **❻** <u>compressibility</u> _____, or tendency

to decrease in volume when pressure is applied. This is because the particles that make up

solids are arranged in a **❼** <u>tightly</u> _____ packed, highly ordered

❽ <u>structural</u> _____ that does not include much free space into

which the particles might be squeezed.

Activity 17
Review of Grammar Topics 6.1–6.5

Seven of the ten sentences contain an error involving one of the grammar topics featured in this unit. Write a C before the three correct sentences. Write X before the incorrect sentences, circle the error, and write a correction above it.

_____ 1. When the schoolchildren visited the museum, their teacher advised him

to be careful.

_____ 2. Do you know were you're going?

_____ 3. Joanne diligently practices her violin everyday because her teacher had

always said that practice makes perfect.

_____ 4. Ernesto graduated from high school at the top of his class, which would

not have happened without his parents' support.

_____ 5. The state enacted a law requiring the prohibition of alcohol in public

facilities, and they were delighted.

_____ 6. When he saw that his cat dropped a half-eaten rat by the door,

Paul flinched.

_____ 7. We're going to the store to pick up groceries for our picnic

_____ 8. Josh is always so happy, especially when he dances wild with his friends.

_____ 9. Coordinating their efforts took a lot of time, but they were delighted

when all of their work had paid off.

_____ 10. Ping-pong might not seem like the most challenging or athletic of sports,

but the athletes who play the game know better.

| Activity 18 | *Editing a Paragraph: Review of Grammar Topics 6.1–6.5* |

Seven of the ten underlined words in this paragraph contain an error involving one of the grammar topics featured in this unit. Correct the errors on the lines provided. If the word or phrase is correct, write C.

When employees fly for their jobs, who should receive the frequent flyer points and free trips that they earn on that airline: the employees or the company? In a ❶ recently _____ meeting, Diana, Jean, and Larry ❷ analyzed _____ the quarterly expense report. "Look at line 415," Diana said. "Air-travel expenses ❸ had increased _____ 28 percent from last year. Is there any room for savings there?"

"Jean and I were discussing that earlier," Larry said. "I think we should begin ❹ requirement _____ our people to join all the frequent-flyer programs so that after they fly 20,000 to 30,000 miles on any one airline, they get a free ticket. Then we should require them to use that free ticket the next time ❺ they _____ have to take a business trip for us."

"I disagree," Jean said. "To begin with, there is no easy way to enforce the ❻ require _____. Who is going to keep track of ❼ exact _____ where each person goes, how many miles each person flies on each airline, and when a free flight coupon is due to that person? It would make us us ❽ appear _____ to be **Big Brother**, looking over their shoulders all the time."

Diana put an end to the discussion. "Both of you think about the matter some more and let me have a memo by next week giving me your position. Then I ❾ decide _____. It is important that ❿ were _____ considering all possible options here."

Big Brother: a phrase describing a government that controls the lives of its citizens

STUDENT ESSAY WRITING

In this section, you will go through the seven steps in writing a five-paragraph narrative essay. To review the details of each step, see Unit 1, pages 8–15.

| Activity 19 | *Original Narrative Essay* |

Using the seven steps that follow, write a five-paragraph narrative essay. Your teacher may assign a topic, you may think of one yourself, or you may choose from the suggestions in Step 1. You might need to do research.

Step 1: Choosing a Topic

Choose a story about your life that you want to share with readers.

Suggestions:

Humanities:	Write a narrative essay describing what experiences led you to choose your college major.
Sciences:	Describe your most interesting experience with science, and explain why you enjoy studying science.
Business:	Describe your experiences in the business world. Did you have a part- or full-time job that encouraged you to major in business in college? Explain how your life experiences have led you to major in business.
Personal:	What is the biggest, most embarrassing mistake you made in your life? What did you learn from this experience?

1. What topic did you choose? _____

2. Why did you choose this topic? _____

_____

_____

Step 2: Brainstorming

Use this space to jot down as many ideas about the topic as you can.

Brainstorming Box

Step 3: Outlining

Prepare a simple outline of your essay. Use the following outline or the outline of narrative elements below it.

Title: _____

I. Introduction _____

    _____

    Background information _____

    _____

    Thesis statement: _____

    _____

II. Point 1

    _____

    _____

III. Point 2

    _____

    _____

IV. Point 3

    _____

    _____

V. Conclusion _____

    _____

Outline of narrative elements:

Setting:

_____

_____

Main characters:

_____

_____

Plot:

_____

_____

Climax:

_____

_____

Ending:

_____

_____

Peer Editing of Outlines

Give your outline to a partner. This space is for your partner to write comments about your outline.

1. Is there anything in the outline that looks unclear to you?

_____

_____

_____

2. Can you think of an area in the outline that needs more development? Do you have any specific suggestions?

_____

_____

_____

3. If you have any other ideas or suggestions, write them here.

_____

_____

_____

Step 4: Writing the First Draft

Use the information from Steps 1–3 to write the first draft of your five-paragraph narrative essay.

Step 5: Peer Editing

Exchange essays with someone else. Read that person's essay and offer feedback on Peer Editing Sheet 6, pages 245–246.

Step 6: Revising Your Draft

Read the comments on Peer Editing Sheet 6 about your essay. Then reread your essay. Can you identify places where you plan to revise? List what you are going to do.

1. _____

_____

_____

2. _____

_____

_____

3. _____

_____

Use all the information from the previous activities to write the final version of your paper. Writers often need to write a third or even a fourth draft to express their ideas as clearly as possible. Write as many drafts as necessary to produce a good essay.

Step 7: Proofing the Final Paper

Be sure to proofread your paper several times before you submit it.

TOPICS FOR WRITING

Here are ten topics for additional persuasive essay writing.

TOPIC 1 ➡ Describe your first trip to the dentist, doctor, or hospital.

TOPIC 2 ➡ Describe your last day of high school.

TOPIC 3 ➡ Describe your adventures on a trip.

TOPIC 4 ➡ Describe a day when something unusual happened where you work.

TOPIC 5 ➡ Describe the day when a best friend moved away.

TOPIC 6 ➡ Describe a situation when your parents punished you.

TOPIC 7 ➡ Describe your proudest moment.

TOPIC 8 ➡ Describe a time when you ended a relationship.

TOPIC 9 ➡ Describe your most embarrassing moment.

TOPIC 10 ➡ Describe a time when you apologized for your actions.

Online Study Center   For additional activities, go to the *Greater Essays* Online Study Center at http://esl.college.hmco.com/pic/greateressays1e

Appendixes

APPENDIX 1

Additional Grammar Practice

Activity 1
Prepositions

Underline the correct preposition in the parentheses.

❶ (In, On) 1812, a collection of fairy tales or folktales was published. These stories became

very popular not only ❷ (at, in) Germany but also throughout Europe and America. The

brothers Jakob and Wilhelm Grimm collected the stories during a period that was characterized

❸ (by, for) a great interest ❹ (for, in) German folklore. Whatever the historical background

of the stories, they have long been a part ❺ (in, of) childhood experience. Children identify

❻ (for, with) the hero, suffer through the inevitable trials and tribulations, and experience

relief and triumph when virtue is finally rewarded. Fairy tales are not only ❼ (for, to) children,

however. Today this fairy tale society, founded ❽ (at, in) 1956 in Germany, has more than

600 members from all over Europe. Scholars publish books ❾ (on, through) fairy tale motifs

and use fairy tales as a source ❿ (of, on) information ⓫ (about, for) life and values

⓬ (in, on) different times and cultures.

Activity 2
Verb Tenses

Underline the correct verb tense in the parentheses.

Carson McCullers left behind an impressive literary legacy when she ❶ (has died, died) at the age of 50 in 1967: five novels, two plays, twenty short stories, two dozen nonfiction pieces, a book of children's verse, and a handful of distinguished poems. Her most acclaimed fiction ❷ (appears, appeared, had appeared) in the 1940s. McCullers was taken for an exceptional writer when she ❸ (publishes, published) *The Heart Is a Lonely Hunter* (1940) at age 23. This work ❹ (is, has) set in a small Southern mill town resembling Columbus, Georgia, where she was born Lula Carson Smith on February 19, 1917. The novel ❺ (reflects, reflected) the author's culture and ❻ (is, will be) her most autobiographical tale.

Activity 3

Editing for Errors

Find these 12 errors and correct them: word form (4), verb tense (3), subject-verb agreement (1), preposition (2), article (2).

Johann Wolfgang von Goethe (1749–1832) was universal genius. He was a poem, novelist,

dramatist, public administrator, and scientist. He had made significant contributions for the

fields of optics, comparative anatomy, and plant morphology. The collected works of this prolific

writer appear in sixty volumes before his death. Goethe is one of the greatest lyric poets, and his

poetry are read and studied today. Modern theaters present his dramatic. His most famous single

work is *Faust*, on which he works his entire lifetime; he published the Part 1 in 1808 and Part 2

in 1832. Early in his career, Goethe was already recognition both in Germany and abroad as

one of the great figures of world literary. He can confidently hold his place with the select

group from Homer, Dante, and Shakespeare.

Activity 4 | **Editing for Specific Errors**

Find these five errors and correct them: subject-verb agreement (2), articles (2), and word form (1).

What is the story behind the origin of the word *asparagus*? This vegetable name have a very

bizarre history. The word *asparagus* means "sparrow grass." What possibility connection could

there be between a sparrow, which is name of a beautiful little brown bird, and this vegetable?

In former times, the people were served asparagus accompanied by cooked sparrows! Because

this green, grasslike vegetable were served with little sparrows, it became known as "sparrow

grass" or asparagus.

Activity 5   **Prepositions**

Complete the paragraph with the words from the box.

as	by	of	in
in	among	of	in

French is widely spoken **1** _____ Africa. The use **2** _____ French as a

common language is a factor of national integration and cohesion where different ethnic

groups have traditionally spoken different languages. Twenty African countries use

French **3** _____ their official language. **4** _____ the most important

French-speaking countries in Africa are Madagascar, Zaire, Senegal, Mali, and Ivory Coast.

Formerly French or Belgian colonies, these countries became independent nations

5 _____ the early 1960s. French is also spoken **6** _____ large segments

of the population **7** _____ the northern African countries **8** _____

Morocco, Algeria, and Tunisia.

Activity 6

Prepositions

Underline the correct preposition in the parentheses.

Chaucer is quite possibly the greatest writer **❶** (at, in, on) English literature. Relatively little

is known **❷** (about, by, to) his early life. He came **❸** (by, from, at) a well-to-do merchant

family that had lived **❹** (at, for, without) several generations in Ipswich, some seventy miles

northeast of London. No school records **❺** (at, by, of) Chaucer have survived. The earliest

known document that names Geoffrey Chaucer is a fragmentary household account book dated

between 1356 and 1359. Chaucer is best known **❻** (for, like, since) his collection of stories

called the *Canterbury Tales*, but this collection **❼** (at, of, with) stories is unfinished.

Activity 7 **Editing Specific Errors**

Five of the eight underlined selections contain errors. Locate and correct the errors.

You put ketchup on French fries and other foods all the time, but did you ever stop to ask

yourself ❶ <u>where this word did come</u> from? Our English word *ketchup* is from the Chinese

word *ke-tsiap*. The Chinese created this great food product in the late seventeenth century. Soon

afterward, British explorers ❷ <u>come</u> across ketchup in nearby Malaysia and brought it back to

the Western world. Fifty years later, this sauce became popular in the American colonies.

Around this time, people realized that tomatoes enhanced ❸ <u>flavor</u> of this sauce, so tomatoes

were ❹ <u>routinely added</u> to ketchup, and red became the ❺ <u>normally</u> color for this sauce.

Oddly enough, ketchup did not ❻ <u>contains</u> any tomatoes until the 1790s ❼ <u>because there</u>

<u>was a mistaken presumption that tomatoes were poisonous</u>! Thus, our English word

ketchup comes from the Chinese name for their original sauce, which was neither red

❽ <u>nor</u> tomato-based.

Activity 8 — Editing Specific Errors

Find these five errors and correct them: number (1), verb tense (1), comma splice (1), preposition (2).

One of the most brilliant composer that the world has ever seen, Franz Schubert (1797–1828), was born in Vienna and lived there until his death. He wrote his first composition in the age of 13 and writes his first symphony at the age of 16. Like Mozart, Schubert was a prolific composer. His list of 998 extant works includes seven masses, nine symphonies, numerous piano pieces, and 606 songs, in a single year, 1815, at the age of 18, he wrote 140 songs. Only a few of Schubert's works were published in his lifetime. He did not profit much from those that he did sell. Like Mozart, he suffered for continuous poverty.

| Activity 9 | **Editing Specific Errors** |

Five of the eight underlined selections contain errors. Locate and correct the errors.

For centuries, ❶ <u>the French universities</u> catered only to the educational needs of the

students, and their buildings were exclusively academic ones. As the number of university

students increased—❷ <u>more than</u> sevenfold between 1950 and 1989—student residences

were added. ❸ <u>In many part of France</u>, the newer city universities were built ❹ <u>in the</u>

<u>suburbs</u>, where land ❺ <u>were less expensive</u>, while the academic buildings remained in the

center of town. In Paris, ❻ <u>for the example</u>, the city university ❼ <u>is location</u> several miles

from the academic Latin Quarter. This creates a serious transportation problem ❽ <u>for the</u>

<u>students</u>, who must commute long distances.

Activity 10 — Prepositions

Complete the paragraph with the words from the box.

in	as	of	for
to	with	to	for

Just as it appears to be, the word *strawberry* is actually a combination **❶** _____

the words *straw* and *berry*. *Straw* here is not the straw you use **❷** _____ drinking;

instead, it refers **❸** _____ dried cut grass. Strawberries grow very close

❹ _____ the ground, and farmers put straw around the plants to keep the

berries off the ground. Coupled **❺** _____ *berry*, the word *straw* indicated the

protective aid so necessary **❻** _____ the successful growth of this fruit. This

combination resulted **❼** _____ *straw berry* (two words). Eventually, this came to be

written **❽** _____ a single word: *strawberry*.

Better Sentence Variety

Many writers do not write well because they do not use a variety of types of sentences. In this appendix, we offer ideas for writing correct sentences of several kinds.

The three sentence types in Appendix 2 are simple, compound, and complex. Good writers use all three types of sentences for a variety of styles.

THE TWO BASIC PARTS OF A SENTENCE

A sentence in English consists of two parts: **subject** and **predicate**. The subject is the part of the sentence that contains who or what the sentence is about. The predicate contains the verb that tells something about the subject.

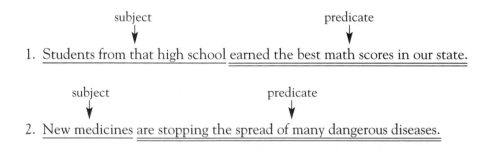

     subject   predicate

1. Students from that high school earned the best math scores in our state.

    subject   predicate

2. New medicines are stopping the spread of many dangerous diseases.

The most important part of the predicate is the **verb**, and the most important part of the subject is the **simple subject**. It is often much easier to find the verb first and then find the subject. In Example 1, the verb is "earned." The complete subject is "students from that high school," but can you find one word that is the central idea of the complete subject? In this case, the simple subject is "students."

In Example 2, the verb is "are stopping." The complete subject is "new medicines." The simple subject is "medicines."

202

Activity 1   **Subjects and Predicates**

Read these five sentences about Coca-Cola. Then draw a line between the complete subject and the complete predicate. The first one has been done for you.

1. The world headquarters of Coca-Cola | is located in Atlanta, Georgia.

2. The Coca-Cola Company produces almost 400 different beverages.

3. The Coca-Cola Company was founded in 1886.

4. Dr. John Stith Pemberton created Coca-Cola.

5. Many years ago, Coca-Cola was marketed as the "Friendliest Drink on Earth."

CLAUSES

A clause is a subject-verb relationship. Each of the following sentences has one subject-verb relationship and therefore one clause:

1. The <u>girls</u> <u>played</u> tennis.

2. The <u>girls and boys</u> <u>played</u> tennis.

3. The <u>girls and boys</u> <u>played</u> tennis and then <u>went</u> to the mall.

Each of the following sentences has two subject-verb relationships and therefore two clauses:

1. The <u>girls</u> <u>played</u> tennis, and the <u>boys</u> <u>went</u> to the mall.

2. The <u>girls and boys</u> <u>played</u> tennis, and then <u>they</u> <u>went</u> to the mall.

Sometimes one clause can be inside another clause. Study this example:

The <u>girls</u> | <u>who</u> <u>played</u> tennis | <u>went</u> to the mall later.

There are two kinds of clauses: **independent** and **dependent**. An independent clause is easy to recognize because it can stand alone. It has meaning all by itself.

Each of the following sentences has one independent clause:

1. The <u>girls</u> <u>played</u> tennis.

2. The <u>girls and boys</u> <u>played</u> tennis.

3. The <u>girls and boys</u> <u>played</u> tennis and then <u>went</u> to the mall.

Each of the following sentences has two independent clauses:

1. The <u>girls</u> played tennis , and the <u>boys</u> went to the mall .

2. The <u>girls and boys</u> played tennis , and then <u>they</u> went to the mall .

In this next example, there are also two clauses, but only one is an independent clause:

The <u>girls</u> <u>who</u> <u>played</u> tennis <u>went</u> to the mall later.

In this sentence, "The girls . . . went to the mall" is an independent clause. The words "who played tennis" also make up a clause but cannot stand alone. This clause has no meaning without the rest of the sentence. We call this kind of clause a *dependent clause* because it depends on the rest of the sentence to have meaning.

The dependent clauses in these sentences have been underlined:

1. The book <u>that I bought</u> is extremely interesting,

2. A bilingual dictionary is ideal for learners <u>whose English is not so good yet.</u>

Activity 2   **Dependent and Independent Clauses**

Read these six sentences about reality television programs. Identify the underlined clauses as either independent (I) or dependent (D).

_____ 1. Reality television programs, <u>which are quite popular,</u> drive my mother crazy.

_____ 2. *Survivor,* <u>which is broadcast on CBS,</u> places castaways in a remote

location and makes them fend for themselves.

_____ 3. *American Idol* is a singing competition that looks for the next vocal

       superstar.

_____ 4. Many of the singers who audition for *American Idol* are not very talented.

_____ 5. Donald Trump's show *The Apprentice*, in which he hires an intern,

       is known for its trademark phrase, "You're fired."

_____ 6. Jasper is a producer for *Big Brother*, which is much more popular in Britain

       than in the United States.

Activity 3	*Independent and Dependent Clauses*

Read these six sentences about Mark Twain. Identify the underlined clauses as either independent (I) or dependent (D).

_____ 1. When Mark Twain was a boy, his family moved to Hannibal, Missouri, where

       he spent many hours playing on the Mississippi River.

_____ 2. *A Connecticut Yankee in King Arthur's Court*, which is one of Twain's most

       popular books, was recently made into a movie.

_____ 3. One of Mark Twain's most famous books is *Huckleberry Finn*, which is a

       story about a young boy and a slave.

_____ 4. Tom Sawyer, whose adventures have delighted many readers, is known for

       his pluck and determination.

_____ 5. Twain's *Life on the Mississippi* describes the adventures that befell him as

       a riverboat pilot.

_____ 6. Mark Twain was born in 1835 and died in 1910, which were both years

       when Halley's Comet was in view.

SENTENCE TYPE 1: SIMPLE SENTENCE

1. A simple sentence has one subject-verb relationship.

   a. I have a cat.

   b. My cat is gray.

   c. The name of my cat begins with the letter B.

2. A simple sentence can have two or more subjects.

   a. France and Germany are located in Europe.

   b. Because of the heavy rains yesterday, Highway 50, Eisenhower Boulevard, and

   Temple Avenue were impassable.

3. A simple sentence can have two or more verbs.

   a. The cat curled up into a ball and went to sleep.

   b. The cat yawned, curled up into a ball, and went to sleep.

Activity 4   **Subjects and Verbs**

Read these sentences about Saturday Night Live. *Underline the subject and draw two lines under the verb.*

1. *Saturday Night Live* has launched the careers of many famous comedians,

   including John Belushi, Eddie Murphy, and Mike Meyers.

2. The weekly guest host of *SNL* plays an active role in picking the skits for

   the show.

3. At the precocious age of seven, Drew Barrymore hosted *SNL*.

4. Lorne Michaels has produced and managed *SNL* for more than twenty-five years.

5. Tina Fey and Amy Poehler serve as the current hosts of *Weekend Update*.

SENTENCE TYPE 2: COMPOUND SENTENCES

1. A compound sentence has two subject-verb relationships.

    a. The <u>rain</u> <u>began</u> to fall, so <u>we</u> <u>stopped</u> playing tennis.

    b. The <u>store</u> <u>had</u> a special sale on children's clothes, and <u>hundreds</u> of parents <u>flocked</u>

    there to shop for bargains.

2. A compound sentence has two subject-verb relationships that are connected
    by a coordinating conjunction. To remember coordinating conjunctions, you
    can use the mnemonic FANBOYS (*for, and, nor, but, or, yet, so*). Of these
    seven coordinating conjunctions, the most commonly used are *and, but,* and *so.*

    a. <u>I</u> will not <u>tell</u> a lie, (for) <u>it</u> would not <u>be</u> honest.

    b. <u>Helen</u> <u>takes</u> the car, (and) <u>she</u> <u>picks up</u> Larry on the way to work.

    c. <u>I</u> would not <u>like</u> to join you for lunch, (nor) would <u>I</u> <u>like</u> to join you for dinner.

    d. <u>Carrie</u> <u>wanted</u> to go to the disco, (but) <u>Francis</u> <u>refused</u> to join her there.

    e. Do <u>I</u> <u>want</u> to go now, (or) do <u>I</u> <u>want</u> to go later?

    f. University <u>students</u> often <u>take</u> an overload of courses, (yet) <u>they</u> <u>should know</u> not

    to overtax themselves.

    g. The <u>teacher</u> <u>prepared</u> her courses the night before, (so) <u>she</u> <u>was ready</u> for

    everything that happened the following day.

| Activity 5 | **Simple and Compound Sentences** |

Read these eight sentences about the Super Bowl. Identify each sentence as simple (S) or compound (C). In compound sentences, circle the coordinating conjunction.

_____ 1. The Super Bowl is one of the biggest sporting events of the year, and it is always one of the most watched television shows of the year.

_____ 2. The Pittsburgh Steelers, the Dallas Cowboys, and the San Francisco Forty-Niners have each won four or more Super Bowls.

_____ 3. Many millions of people watch the Super Bowl on television, and many companies therefore spend millions of dollars advertising their products during the show.

_____ 4. One of the most famous commercials ever shown during the Super Bowl was a Nike commercial modeled on George Orwell's book *1984*.

_____ 5. The Buffalo Bills lost four Super Bowls in a row, and this accomplishment makes them one of the saddest footnotes in Super Bowl history.

_____ 6. New Orleans, Jacksonville, and Houston have all hosted the Super Bowl, which brings in millions of dollars to the local economies.

_____ 7. Other major sporting events include the Stanley Cup for hockey, Wimbledon for tennis, and the World Series for baseball.

_____ 8. Many people would like to attend the championship games of major sporting teams, but the tickets are quite expensive.

| Activity 6 | **Identifying Compound Sentences** |

Read these sentences about the great writer Geoffrey Chaucer. Underline the two compound sentences.

Chaucer is quite possibly the greatest writer of English literature. He was most likely born in the early 1340s, and he died in 1400. Relatively little is known about his early life. He came from a well-to-do merchant family that had lived for several generations in Ipswich, some seventy miles northeast of London. No school records of Chaucer have survived. The earliest known document that bears the name of Geoffrey Chaucer is a fragmentary household account book dated between 1356 and 1359. Chaucer is best known for his collection of stories called the *Canterbury Tales*, but this collection of stories is unfinished.

| Activity 7 | *Identifying Compound Sentences* |

Read these sentences from an essay in Unit 6. Underline the two compound sentences.

When my maternal grandparents would fly from North America to South America to visit us, my mother had to translate among the different family members. We spoke Spanish in our house, and my American grandparents spoke only English. Since they did not speak a word of Spanish, my mother was constantly interpreting questions and answers. With my mom's help, I could understand my grandparents, but I wanted to be able to speak to them by myself.

Activity 8	Original Compound Sentences

Write five compound sentences. Use a different connector in each one.

1. _____

   _____

2. _____

   _____

3. _____

   _____

4. _____

   _____

5. _____

   _____

SENTENCE TYPE 3: COMPLEX SENTENCES

1. A complex sentence has at least one independent clause and one dependent clause.

   a. **The professor returned the examination** that we took last Wednesday.

   b. **The examination** that we took last Wednesday **was very difficult.**

   c. **The examination was difficult** because it had more than fifty questions.

2. The clauses are joined by a subordinating conjunction (*because, after, although, that, who*).

   a. **The house sustained some damage** because the wind was very strong in this area.

   b. After the house sustained some damage, **we planned some repairs.**

   c. **The dictionary** that you bought **is excellent.**

Activity 9	Identifying Independent and Dependent clauses

Read the following eight sentences about inventions. Each one is a complex sentence. Draw two lines under the independent clause and one line under the dependent clause. The first one has been done for you.

1. The electric light bulb that we depend on every night for light was invented in 1900.

2. Because the Internet is useful and practical, it has caught on rapidly with all ages.

3. Although people complain about high gas prices, no one has invented a fuel-free vehicle yet.

4. Do you know the name of the person who invented the radio?

5. One of the most important inventions that we use every day without thinking has to be the simple ink pen.

6. When electricity was invented, many people were afraid to have it in their houses.

7. How did people in warm climates survive before air conditioning was invented?

8. When bubbles were added to Coca-Cola, this drink began to catch on.

SENTENCE VARIETY: ADD ADJECTIVES

Adding adjectives to sentences is one of the best ways to improve sentences. Adjectives can add color and vigor to uninteresting sentences. Adjectives are usually placed in front of nouns.

> *Good:* The wind blew across the lake.

> *Better:* The **cold** wind blew across the **frozen** lake.

| **Activity 10** | **Original Writing with Adjectives** |

Add adjectives on the lines to improve this story.

Once upon a time, there was a / an _____ monster that lived in a / an

_____ forest. The monster was _____. One day, the

monster met a / an _____ frog. When the monster asked the frog whether he

was ugly, the frog replied, "You are not ugly. You are _____." The monster

and frog then became friends and soon met a / an _____ princess. Since

the princess was _____, she immediately told them that they were

both _____. The _____ monster, _____

frog, and _____ princess soon became _____ allies.

| **Activity 11** | **Order of Adjectives** |

Read the following sentences about persuasive writing. Write the words in the correct order.

1. writing persuasive	4. set exercises next the of
2. people other	5. brief a essay
3. view our point unique of	6. given a subject

Much of the writing that we do is persuasive. In ❶ _____

_____, we encourage ❷ _____

to see ❸ _____. In the model essay,

the writer wants to convince the reader that spam should be outlawed.

Through ❹ _____, you will go through

the process of writing ❺ _____

in which you try to persuade your reader to agree with you on

❻ _____.

Activity 12   *Order of Adjectives*

Read these sentences about the composer Franz Schubert. Write the words in the correct order.

1. the most brilliant composers	5. pieces numerous piano
2. first composition his	6. works only few Schubert's a of
3. his symphony first	7. poverty continuous
4. a prolific composer	

One of ❶ _____ that the world has

ever seen, Franz Schubert (1797–1828), was born in Vienna and lived there until his death. He

wrote ❷ _____ at the age of 13 and

wrote ❸ _____ at the age of 16.

Like Mozart, Schubert was ❹ _____ .

His   list   of   998   extant   works   includes   seven   masses,   nine   symphonies,

❺ _____ , and 606 songs. In a single year,

1815, at the age of 18, he wrote 140 songs. ❻ _____

_____ were published in his lifetime. Nor did he profit much from those that he did

sell. Like Mozart, he suffered from ❼ _____ .

Activity 13   *Adjectives in Real-World Sentences*

Copy five sentences from a novel, a magazine, a newspaper, or the Internet. Circle all the adjectives.

1. _____

_____

2. _____

_____

3. _____

_____

4. _____

_____

5. _____

_____

Activity 14   *Adding Adjectives to Improve Sentences*

Write five sentences without adjectives. Then write the same sentences with adjectives. For variety, add at least two adjectives to some of your new sentences.

1. Good: _____

_____

Better: _____

_____

2. Good: _____

_____

Better: _____

_____

3. Good: _____

_____

Better: _____

_____

4. Good: _____

_____

Better: _____

_____

5. Good: _____

_____

Better: _____

_____

PREPOSITIONAL PHRASES

Another easy way to add variety to your sentences is to add prepositional phrases. A prepositional phrase consists of a preposition and an object (a noun or a pronoun). Study these examples:

1. A new ambassador **to a foreign country** must learn the customs **of this country**

   quite quickly.

2. When I first got an e-mail account ten years ago, I received communications

   only **from** friends, family, and professional acquaintances.

Notice that the next example has twenty-five words, but only two of the words are not in a prepositional phrase:

> 3. **With** the discovery **of** oil **in** Alaska **in** the early 1900s, thousands **of people**
>
> flocked **to that area for the prospect of** a better economic future.

Prepositional phrases can serve all sorts of purposes. For example, prepositional phrases can tell *where* (in the kitchen), *when* (in the late seventeenth century), and *why* (for a better life).

Perhaps the most commonly used prepositions are *at, on, in, for, before, after, with,* and *without.* Here is a larger list:

about	besides	in lieu of	regarding
above	between	in place of	since
according to	beyond	including	through
across	by	inside	throughout
after	concerning	instead of	till
against	contrary to	into	to
ahead of	despite	like	toward
along	down	near	under
among	due to	next to	underneath
around	during	of	until
at	except	off	up
because of	for	on	upon
before	from	on account of	versus
behind	in	out	via
below	in addition to	outside	with
beneath	in back of	over	without
beside	in front of	past	

Activity 15   *Identifying Prepositional Phrases*

Read these paragraphs about a famous landmark in California. Underline the prepositional phrases and draw a circle around the prepositions.

Millions of people all over the world have seen the Golden Gate Bridge in San Francisco, so people now equate the Golden Gate Bridge with the city of San Francisco. Although they know that the Golden Gate Bridge is in San Francisco, what they do not know is that the nickname of this structure was "the bridge that couldn't be built." The idea of the construction of a bridge across San Francisco Bay had been discussed for years before the construction of the Golden Gate Bridge was actually started in 1933. For a variety of reasons, this bridge was long considered impossible to build.

First of all, the weather in the area—with high winds, rain, and fog—was rarely good. Second, engineers thought that the strong ocean currents in the bay meant that the bridge could not be built. Furthermore, they were worried about how the strong winds in the area would affect any large structure. Finally, it was the Depression. The poor economy was causing people to experience incredible difficulties, so many people thought that it would be foolish to spend such a large amount of money on such an impossible project.

Word Parts (Suffixes)

Studying word parts will help you to figure out new words and increase your academic vocabulary.

ADJECTIVE ENDINGS

Ending	Meaning	Examples
-able / -ible	able to	likable, flexible
-al	having the quality of	optional, original
-ant	having the quality of	pleasant, resultant
-ar / -ary	related to	muscular, culinary
-ed	past participle	delighted, surprised
-en	made of	golden, wooden
-ent	having the quality of	apparent, insistent
-esque	in the style of	grotesque, picturesque
-ful	full of	careful, mindful
-ing	present participle	amazing, distressing,
-ive	tending to	creative, destructive

-less	without	aim<u>less</u>, hope<u>less</u>
-like	like, similar to	child<u>like</u>, lady<u>like</u>
-ly	having the qualities of	friend<u>ly</u>, man<u>ly</u>
-ory	related to	obliga<u>tory</u>, sens<u>ory</u>
-ous / -ious	full of	fam<u>ous</u>, relig<u>ious</u>
-proof	protected from	fire<u>proof</u>, water<u>proof</u>
-ward	in the direction of	back<u>ward</u>, down<u>ward</u>
-y	related to	laz<u>y</u>, wind<u>y</u>

NOUN ENDINGS

Ending	Meaning	Examples
-an / -ian	person related to	Americ<u>an</u>, guard<u>ian</u>
-ance / -ence	condition, state	relev<u>ance</u>, exist<u>ence</u>
-ant / -ent	person who	entr<u>ant</u>, stud<u>ent</u>
-ation	action, state	communic<u>ation</u>, explan<u>ation</u>
-ee	person who receives something	less<u>ee</u>, trust<u>ee</u>
-er / -or	person who does	bak<u>er</u>, sail<u>or</u>
-ese	person related to	Japan<u>ese</u>, Taiwan<u>ese</u>
-hood	state of	neighbor<u>hood</u>, parent<u>hood</u>
-ics	science, art or practice	phys<u>ics</u>, statist<u>ics</u>
-ing	gerund (action)	danc<u>ing</u>, read<u>ing</u>
-ion / -sion / -tion	action, state, result	un<u>ion</u>, conclu<u>sion</u>, reac<u>tion</u>
-ist	person who believes/does	commun<u>ist</u>, typ<u>ist</u>
-ment	result of action	docu<u>ment</u>, place<u>ment</u>

-ness	quality, state	friend<u>liness</u>, trustworth<u>iness</u>
-ship	condition, quality	friend<u>ship</u>, leader<u>ship</u>
-ty / -ity	quality, condition	dens<u>ity</u>, equal<u>ity</u>

VERB ENDINGS

Ending	Meaning	Examples
-ate	cause, make	calcul<u>ate</u>, demonstr<u>ate</u>
-en	made of, make	fatt<u>en</u>, short<u>en</u>
-ify	make	clar<u>ify</u>, terr<u>ify</u>
-ize	make	demon<u>ize</u>, plagiar<u>ize</u>

ADVERB ENDINGS

Ending	Meaning	Examples
-ly	manner of	careful<u>ly</u>, unequivocal<u>ly</u>

EXAMPLES OF WORD FORMS ACROSS PARTS OF SPEECH

Noun	Verb	Adjective	Adverb
action	act	active	actively
benefit	benefit	beneficial	beneficially
care	care	careful	carefully
		caring	caringly
difference	differ	different	differently
persuasion	persuade	persuasive	persuasively
temptation	tempt	tempting	temptingly

Sentence Problems: Fragments, Run-ons, Comma Splices

Three common sentence problems are fragments, run-ons, and comma splices.

WHAT IS A FRAGMENT?

A fragment is an incomplete sentence.

1. Running as fast as he can

2. The house at the end of the block

3. Make a medical breakthrough

All complete sentences must contain a subject and a verb. These fragments can be turned into complete sentences rather easily.

1. He is running as fast as he can.

2. The house at the end of the block belongs to the Meyers.

3. The research teams hope to make a medical breakthrough.

Sometimes fragments contain a subject and a verb, but they are dependent clauses. When a fragment is incorrectly separated from an independent clause, either the dependent clause must be made into a complete sentence or the dependent clause must be attached to an independent clause.

Fragment / dependent clause: Because I studied so hard last night.

Independent clause: I studied so hard last night.

Combined clauses: Because I studied so hard last night, I easily passed my exam.

Fragment/dependent clause: After Juanita danced with Sebastian.

Independent clause: Juanita danced with Sebastian.

Combined clauses: After Juanita danced with Sebastian, Helen stormed out of the room.

Activity I	Identifying Fragments

Identify each as a sentence (S) or a fragment (F).

___S, F___ 1. Jason went to the store and bought onions. Not realizing at the time that he needed ginger as well.

_____ 2. Making her decision carefully. Pamela ordered two cups of coffee. Hoping her friend would arrive on time.

_____ 3. We will first take the children to the zoo, and then we will go to dinner.

_____ 4. As summer vacation comes closer, I find myself planning a trip to the Caribbean. To think about this makes me happy.

_____ 5. I cannot believe what Sheila did, and I am not happy about it!

_____ 6. I still love my old pony. Although it does not run that fast.

_____ 7. With my father nearby, I reached for the broom. Leaning over too far caused me to fall.

_____ 8. They were all having a good time. Even the grown-ups.

Activity 2	Correcting Fragments

Rewrite the four fragments from Activity 1 so that they are correct sentences.

1. _____

   _____

2. _____

   _____

3. _____

   _____

4. _____

   _____

Activity 3	Identifying and Correcting Fragments

Read this paragraph. Underline the one fragment. On the lines below, rewrite the sentence to eliminate the fragment.

The café plays an important role in the daily life of the French people. Students go there at any time of day not only to have something to eat or drink but also to relax, to read the paper, or to listen to music. Since many students live quite a distance from the university and since the existing libraries are often overcrowded. The café also offers a place to study. For many young people, the café is the ideal spot to meet one's friends or to strike up a casual conversation with other students. Most French cafés are divided into two parts: the inside section and the terrace, which extends onto the sidewalk. In spring and summer, most customers prefer the terrace, where they can enjoy the good weather and observe the people walking by.

_____

_____

| Activity 4 | *Identifying and Correcting Fragments* |

Read this paragraph. Underline the two fragments. On the lines below, rewrite them to eliminate the fragments.

I read two books on business communication. The first book, *Effective Business Communication*, is an essential resource on business correspondence for the modern office. In today's business climate, revolutionized by electronic mail and overnight package delivery. It is important to communicate clearly and precisely in writing. *Effective Business Communication* offers sound advice for business writers; it is comprehensive yet concise. The second book is *Business Writing for Today*. Also claims to be an essential source on business correspondence for today's business world. However, this book is not as well-written or as comprehensive. *Business Writing for Today* discusses a few aspects of e-mail that are not covered in *Effective Business Communication*. The authors then move on to samples of business correspondence, but these samples lack any information about the senders' reasons for writing these letters. Therefore, it is my opinion that *Effective Business Communication* would certainly be a more valuable resource guide to have in the office than *Business Writing for Today*.

1. _____

_____

_____

2. _____

_____

_____

| **Activity 5** | *Identifying and Correcting Fragments* |

Read this paragraph. Underline the two fragments. On the lines below, rewrite them to eliminate the fragments.

French is widely spoken in Africa. The use of French as a common language is a factor of national integration and cohesion. Where different ethnic groups have traditionally spoken different languages. Twenty African countries use French as their official language. Among the most important French-speaking countries in Africa are Madagascar, Zaire, Senegal, Mali, and Ivory Coast. Formerly French or Belgian colonies. These countries became independent nations in the early 1960s. French is also spoken by large segments of the population in the northern African countries of Morocco, Algeria, and Tunisia.

1. _____

   _____

   _____

2. _____

   _____

   _____

Activity 6   *Identifying and Correcting Fragments*

Read this paragraph. Underline the two fragments. On the lines below, rewrite them to eliminate the fragments.

Chaucer was likely born in the early 1340s and died in 1400. Is quite possibly the greatest writer of English literature. Relatively little is known about his early life. He came from a well-to-do merchant family that lived for several generations in Ipswich, some seventy miles northeast of London. No school records of Chaucer have survived. The earliest known document that names Geoffrey Chaucer is a fragmentary household account book. Dated between 1356 and 1359. Chaucer is best known for his collection of stories called the *Canterbury Tales*, but this collection of stories is unfinished.

1. _____

_____

_____

2. _____

_____

_____

Activity 9	*Identifying and Correcting Run-On Problems*

Read this paragraph about a well-known author. Underline the two run-ons. On the lines below, rewrite the sentences so that they are correct.

Carson McCullers left behind an impressive literary legacy, she died at the age of 50 in 1967. Her work included five novels, two plays, twenty short stories, some two dozen nonfiction pieces, a book of children's verse, and a handful of distinguished poems. Her most acclaimed fiction appeared in the 1940s. McCullers was taken for an exceptional writer at the age of just 23. That was when she published *The Heart Is a Lonely Hunter* (1940), which is set in a small Southern mill town resembling Columbus, Georgia, where she was born on February 19, 1917. People loved this novel, the novel accurately reflects the author's culture and is her most autobiographical tale.

1. _____

_____

_____

2. _____

_____

_____

WHAT IS A COMMA SPLICE?

A comma splice is a special kind of run-on sentence in which two independent clauses are joined by a comma. Unfortunately, a comma is not strong enough for this task. Independent clauses must be joined by a semicolon or by a comma and a conjunction.

Activity 10   Identifying Comma Splice Problems

Identify each as a sentence (S) or a comma splice (CS).

_____ 1. It is really hot outside today, let's go swimming.

_____ 2. Patsy asked me to join her, and I said that I would.

_____ 3. The jury returned a guilty verdict; the defendant sobbed.

_____ 4. On *The Simpsons*, Ned Flanders is the Simpsons' next door neighbor,
Homer annoys Ned all the time.

_____ 5. Cell phones are becoming increasingly popular, and land lines will likely
become less and less popular.

_____ 6. My little sister is always cajoling me to help her with her homework, but I
encourage her to do it on her own.

_____ 7. My friend Harry will never go to a movie by himself, I go to movies by
myself all the time.

_____ 8. I enjoy cooking a lot, seafood is my favorite cuisine.

Activity 11   Correcting Comma Splice Problems

Rewrite the four comma splices from Activity 10 so that they are correct sentences.

1. _____

_____

2. _____

_____

3. _____

_____

4. _____

_____

APPENDIX 5

Preposition Combinations

VERB + PREPOSITION

account for	consist of	pay for
agree on	count on	rely on
agree with	depend on	stop from
apply for	hear about	substitute for
approve of	hear from	talk to
belong to	listen to	think about
care about	look at	think of
complain about	look for	wait for
comply with		

ADJECTIVE + PREPOSITION

accustomed to	bad at	different from
acquainted with	bored with	disappointed with/in/by
afraid of	capable of	doubtful about
answerable to	connected to/with	enthusiastic about
attached to	delighted at/about	envious of
aware of	dependent on	excited about

famous for	proud of	similar to
guilty of	related to	suitable for
interested in	responsible for	suspicious of
opposed to	satisfied with	typical of
pleased with	serious about	used to
popular with		(= accustomed to)

NOUN + PREPOSITION

advantage of	increase/decrease in, of	order for
application for	invitation to	price of
benefit of	interest in	reason for
cause of	lack of	reply to
cost of	matter with	request for
demand for	need for	solution to
difference between	opinion of	trouble with
example of		

Peer Editing Sheets

Peer Editor: _____

Writer: _____

1. What is the general topic of the essay? _____

   _____

2. How many paragraphs are there? _____

3. Do you think the introduction does a good job of introducing the topic? _____

   Explain your answer briefly. _____

   _____

4. Can you identify the thesis statement? Write it here. _____

   _____

   _____

5. Did you find any examples of *this* or *these* as connectors? Write up to three examples here.

   _____

   _____

   _____

6. If you found any spelling errors, write one of them here. _____

   _____

7. If you found any grammar errors, write one of them here. _____

   _____

8. Do you agree with the writer's presentation on his/her topic? _____ Why or why not? Give

examples of things you agree or disagree with. _____

_____

_____

_____

_____

PEER EDITING SHEET #2   **UNIT 2, Activity 19, page 56**
Process Essay, Step 5

Peer Editor: _____

Writer: _____

1. What process does this essay describe? _____

   _____

2. How many paragraphs are there? _____

3. Organization: How many body paragraphs are there? _____ Does each body paragraph

   have a good topic sentence? _____ If you can suggest improvements for one of the topic

   sentences, write your suggestion here. _____

   _____

   _____

4. Organization: How is the essay organized? (circle one)   **chronologically**   or   **by priority**?

5. Are the steps of the process in logical order? _____ If not, explain your answer here.

   _____

   _____

   _____

6. Organization: Were any steps left out that you think should be included? _____ If so,

   write that step here and put a star (*) in the essay to show where the step should be inserted.

   _____

   _____

7. Language: Did the writer use any time words as transitions? If so, circle them in the essay. If not, mark any places where time words would be helpful.

8. Language: If you found any spelling errors, write one of them here. _____

9. Language: Look for grammar errors, especially those relating to Grammar Topics 2.1–2.5 in this unit. If you found any grammar errors, write one of them here. _____

_____

10. Vocabulary: Can you find two words or phrases that make the essay sound advanced? If not, can you suggest two such vocabulary words and tell where they should be placed in the essay?

_____

_____

PEER EDITING SHEET #3 **UNIT 3, Activity 19, page 90**
Comparison/Contrast Essay, Step 5

Peer Editor: _____

Writer: _____

1. In a few words, what is the essay about? _____

   _____

2. How many paragraphs are there? _____

3. Organization: Which method of organization is used? (circle one)   **block**   or   **point-by-point**

4. Does the writer believe that there are more similarities or more differences between the

   two subjects? _____

5. Can you identify the thesis statement? Write it here. _____

   _____

   _____

6. Language: Comparison-contrast essays often use transitions such as *like, similar to, whereas,* and

   unlike. Write two or three examples of comparison-contrast transitions that you found in this

   essay. (If you did not find any, mark places in the essay where transitions would be helpful.)

   _____

   _____

   _____

7. Support: Are the comparisons supported with sufficient and appropriate details? _____

   If not, put a star (*) next to the places that need supporting information.

8. Language: Look for grammar errors, especially those relating to Grammar Topics 3.1–3.5 in this unit. If you found any grammar errors, write one of them here. _____

9. Sentence structure: One of the worst and most easily corrected composition errors is the fragment. (See Appendix 4, page 221.) Does this essay have any fragments? _____ If so, write FRAG by it on the essay and write a possible correction here. _____

_____

_____

10. Organization: Does the writer restate the thesis in the conclusion? _____ If not, make a note of this on the essay draft.

PEER EDITING SHEET #4   **UNIT 4, Activity 19, page 122**
                              Cause-Effect Essay, Step 5

Peer Editor: _____

Writer: _____

1. What is the general topic of the essay? _____

   _____

2. How many paragraphs are there? _____

3. Content: Do you agree with the writer's logic and the information in this essay? Explain your

   answer briefly. _____

   _____

   _____

   _____

4. Organization: What kind of organization is used: focus-on-effects or focus-on-causes?

   _____

5. Organization: Fill in the blanks to illustrate the organization of this essay.

   CAUSE: _____

   EFFECTS: _____, _____, _____

                                    OR

   EFFECT: _____

   CAUSES: _____, _____, _____

6. Language: Write three to five examples of transitions and connectors that indicate a cause-effect essay. If there are none, suggest one or two places where they could be added.

_____

_____

_____

7. Language: Look for grammar errors, especially those relating to Grammar Topics 4.1–4.5 in this unit. If you found any grammar errors, write one of them here. _____

_____

8. Supporting details: In your opinion, are the three causes or three effects believable to you? Does the writer give sufficient support for each of these? Explain your answer. _____

_____

_____

_____

_____

PEER EDITING SHEET #5   **UNIT 5, Activity 20, page 155**
Persuasive Essay, Step 5

Peer Editor: _____

Writer: _____

1. In your own words, what is the main point of this essay? In other words, what is the author's

    position on the issue? _____

    _____

    _____

2. Supporting details: Examine the writer's supporting evidence. What do you think is the writer's

    most convincing point in the essay? _____

    _____

    _____

3. Which of the author's points is the least convincing? How could this point be improved?

    _____

    _____

    _____

4. Has this essay changed your opinion about this issue? Why or why not?

    _____

    _____

    _____

5. Language: Look for grammar errors, especially those relating to Grammar Topics 5.1–5.5 in this unit. If you found any grammar errors, write one of them here. _____

_____

_____

6. Vocabulary: Can you find two words or phrases that make the essay sound advanced? If not, can you suggest two such vocabulary words and tell where they should be placed in the essay?

_____

_____

_____

PEER EDITING SHEET #6   **UNIT 6, Activity 19, page 189**
Narrative Essay, Step 5

Peer Editor: _____

Writer: _____

1. What is the general topic of the essay? _____

_____

2. How many paragraphs are there? _____

3. In your opinion, what are the three most memorable details in the essay? Do not look back at

the essay.

   a. _____

   b. _____

   c. _____

4. Do you think the introduction does a good job of introducing the topic? In other words, is there a

good hook? _____ Explain your answer briefly. _____

_____

_____

5. Language: Does the writer use the past tense correctly? _____ Use a highlighter to mark

places where there is a problem with a past tense.

6. Language: Look for other grammar errors, especially those relating to Grammar Topics 6.1–6.5 in

this unit. If you found any grammar errors, write one of them here.

_____

_____

7. Language: Write three interesting or especially descriptive adjectives that the writer included in the

essay. _____ , _____ , _____

8. In a narrative, it is important for the information to be in the correct sequence. Does the writer tell

the story in the correct order? _____ If not, write a comment here to help the writer put the

information in a better order. _____

_____

_____

9. Do you have any other comments about the essay? Do you have any suggestions for improving the

essay? _____

_____

_____

_____

_____

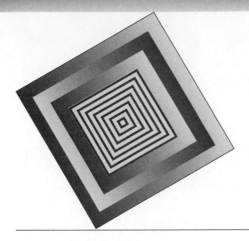

Index